THE POSTAGE STAMP GARDEN BOOK

HOW TO GROW ALL THE FOOD YOU CAN EAT IN VERY LITTLE SPACE

BY DUANE NEWCOMB

ILLUSTRATED BY BARBARA BRODY

Published by J.P. Tarcher, Inc., Los Angeles

Distributed by Hawthorn Books, Inc., New York

Copyright © 1975 by Duane G. Newcomb
All rights reserved
Library of Congress Catalog Card Number: 74-23021

ISBN: 0-87477-035-1

Manufactured in the United States of America

Designed and typeset by Freedmen's Organization
418 South Western Ave., Los Angeles, California 90020

Published by J. P. Tarcher, Inc.
9110 Sunset Blvd., Los Angeles, California 90069

Published simultaneously in Canada by
Prentice-Hall of Canada, Ltd.
1870 Birchmount Road, Scarborough, Ontario

2 3 4 5 6 7 8 9 0

Table of Contents

In the 1890s, outside Paris, a few enterprising Frenchmen began raising crops using a new method all their own. Over their land they spread an 18-inch layer of manure (plentiful in the day of the horse and buggy) and planted their vegetables so close together in this rich material that the leaves touched one another as the plants grew. Under this carpet of leaves the ground remained moist, warm, and vigorous. During periods of frost in early springtime, they set glass jars over the tiny plants to give them an early start. So good were the Frenchmen in devising fresh ways of growing things that they got in nine crops each year.

Such was the birth of the French Intensive method of gardening, an early form of what we now call the organic method.

In the following two decades there developed another organic gardening movement. In Switzerland, a remarkable philosopher from Austria, Rudolf Steiner, was founding a new spiritual or psychic philosophy and setting up a variety of schools and centers dedicated to seeking a larger understanding of the balance of nature. He and his followers did research in education, the handicapped, medical therapy, science and mathematics, art, architecture, sculpture, music, speech, and other fields, including farming and gardening. He became convinced that Europe's crops were declining in nutrients and yields and that the cause lay in the inorganic chemical fertilizers and pesticides that were being recklessly introduced at the time. All the synthetic chemicals, he believed, were contaminating the soil, destroying its natural texture, and killing microorganisms and friendly animals and insects necessary for the balance of nature.

Steiner and his followers developed a gardening method called "bio-dynamic." They emphasized the exclusive and balanced use of organic fertilizers—composted leaves, grass, manure, and so on. They investigated what is now called companion planting—finding that certain plants (like beans and cabbages) do better when grown together and that some plants (like beans and onions) do worse. They also sought new ways of arranging crops in the field. They recognized that the old irrigation techniques, in which the rows between vegetables were flooded, submerged the roots in water and eroded the soil. People walked through these rows, compacting the earth still more. Moisture, soil aeration, soil texture, all important to growth, were haphazard and constantly fluctuating. Thus these biodynamic gardeners hit upon the idea of planting in mounded beds that permitted adequate drainage and that were narrow enough so that a person didn't have to walk or trundle carts over them.

Between the 1930s and the 1960s, an Englishman, Alan Chadwick, set out to combine the French Intensive and biodynamic methods and to add to them various ideas of his own, such as planting by the phases of the moon. In the 1960s he brought his meld of techniques to America, to the four-acre Garden Project at the University of California at Santa Cruz. The acreage that he began with had hard, clayey, "impossible" soil, in which even weeds failed to grow. In one season, using simple hand tilling and organic materials, Chadwick and his students brought the acreage to fertility. In a few seasons they had the richest, most beautiful gardens around.

The intensive method that Chadwick and his students used—and still use—produces four times as many vegetables per acre as those produced by commerical farmers using mechanical and chemical techniques. They also use half the water and far less of the back-breaking energy expended by regular farmers. The vegetables are wonderfully plump and tasty and nutritious.

In this book I borrow from these organic and intensive methods, as well as from others, and adapt them for use by the home gardener in his backyard. I have followed none of the systems exactly, but have modified them whenever necessary to take into account the practical needs of the home gardener who wants an easy way to get good results and lacks time and space for involved methods or systems. This book offers simple, easy methods that work—and that can be bountiful beyond one's dreams.

My own experience in growing vegetables the organic, intensive way over the years has been a happy one, full of surprising results. I hope that the reader will try the intensive methods, do some gardening of postage-stamp size, and then do some experimenting of his own. Then he can experience at long last a similar feeling about growing his own on his own soil, with wondrous results.

I wish to thank the publisher and the editor for their encouragement and suggestions and to thank the illustrator, Barbara Brody, for her sprightly and imaginative drawings.

Duane G. Newcomb

CHAPTER ONE

So You Want To Grow Vegetables

Even as a failed gardener, I loved to grow vegetables!

Every year on the first warm day of spring I rushed outdoors to spade up the backyard and plant as many different kinds of vegetables as I possibly could. Afterwards I would stand at the edge of the freshly raked garden and visualize the hoards of peas, carrots, tomatoes, and other vegetables that would soon be growing there.

Unfortunately (until a few years ago) that's where reality ended. For although I was good at visualizing vegetables, I wasn't very good at growing them. And to me that was a great tragedy because I really tried. I'd received degrees in both botany and forestry. I read the latest scientific bulletins on vegetable gardening. I knew what the insides of a carrot looked like, how to develop new varieties of plants from old, what macro- and micronutrients were, and what the names of all the major plant diseases were and how to identify them. Yet with

1

all this superior knowledge, I couldn't grow a vegetable garden worthy of the name.

My beets came up in clumps, then died. My carrots either didn't show up at all or turned out small and spindly. My bean pods shriveled up at the ends. The birds ate all my baby cucumber plants. And many of the vegetables that did grow were stunted.

In short, I had a brown thumb.

Practically anybody could do a better job than I did. Two small boys down the street grew squash three times larger than mine; and my father-in-law, who'd never taken a botany course in his life and didn't know an annual from a perennial, kept bringing me great quantities of vegetables from his garden that not only were bigger than mine but tasted better too.

I was starting to get a complex about it.

Then one day a few years ago, one of my friends who had come by for a cup of coffee took one look at my garden and started telling me about the "new" French Intensive gardening method that he'd heard about. The intensive method had been used in Europe for many years, but had just recently been introduced in the western United States. The main points that stuck in my mind were: lots of vegetables in a small space, plants all together, little weeding, mounded beds. . . . My visions were returning.

I didn't need much urging to give it a try. I talked to everyone I knew who had some information on the system. I sent for general literature on organic gardening. I read everything I could find on the French Intensive method itself (which wasn't much), and then I started.

My space was small and odd-shaped, so I modified the method to fit my own garden, utilizing eight 4-by-4-foot beds. I dug up the beds according to the methods that I had learned about, watered, planted the seeds, and waited. Within a few days there were tiny plants popping through the ground everywhere. I'd gotten my garden to this point many times before only to have my vegetables die or turn out badly. So I waited and watched as they began to grow, knowing, just knowing, that something bad was bound to happen. This time, however, nothing failed. Nature and I, hand in hand, had triumphed. Every vegetable came up just as it was supposed to. The yields were tremendous. One 4-by-4-foot bed yielded a thousand carrots. I produced oodles of tomatoes, spinach, peas, beans, and cabbage.

Since that memorable summer I've discovered that I can grow (and my friends can grow) surprising quantities of vegetables in a very small space with little work. And now that's what I'm going to show you how to do in this book, in what I call Intensive Postage Stamp gardens. That's IPS gardens for short.

The IPS garden that we will make here generally won't use pure French Intensive methods since I don't feel that these methods entirely suit the needs of the average person who wants to garden. Instead, it will consist of a combination of that system along with bits and pieces of other intensive methods that I and other gardeners have used successfully.

I now know that, no matter what the conditions, vegetable gardening doesn't have to be a problem and that anyone who can turn over a shovelful of dirt can grow almost anything he or she wants to. Give me a season and you'll know it too.

This book itself is in no sense technical. In every instance, it emphasizes the easy way to do the job. In some cases I'll show you several ways to do something so that you can garden like the experts or adjust their methods to fit whatever conditions you find in your own garden. When I talk about compost, for instance, I'll show you how to make a compost that even the most finicky of gardeners would be proud of; or, if you'd rather not bother, we'll do it the easy way using a garbage can in the garage. In all cases the instructions will be simple. After all, there's nothing difficult about gardening.

And although I am a botanist, don't hold that against me. I've had as much trouble learning how to grow good vegetables as almost anyone I know. And after having tried and failed many times, then finally mastered the ins and outs of superior vegetable gardening in a small space, I'd like to pass this knowledge on to you. Hopefully, I can spare you many of the disappointing experiences that I went through.

Moreover, I'd like to share with you the fun and emotional experience that vegetable gardening really is. There's something about it that fills you with pride and a sense of accomplishment. When in my first year of IPS gardening, I picked the first big, ripe, juicy tomato of the season, I was so proud of what I'd done that I refused to let anyone cut it up until I'd paraded it around the entire neighborhood so that everyone else could see. And when I had to quit gardening for the winter, I could hardly wait until spring so that I could start growing things again. Believe me, it's that infectious. . . .

Now let's take a brief look at the general principles of IPS gardening. Then in a later chapter we'll learn exactly how to put them to use in our own gardens.

Lots of Vegetables in a Very Small Space

IPS gardens use all available garden space by eliminating rows and growing most vegetables a few inches apart across the entire bed. Every last inch of soil is utilized. In a one-square-foot IPS garden you can grow about as many carrots as you can in a 12-foot row in a conventional garden. Other vegetables give similar results depending on the spacing. For this reason you can easily produce an abundant supply of your favorite vegetables in a space so small that you ordinarily wouldn't even consider it adequate for gardening.

Less Weeding and Watering

The overlapping leaves of vegetables planted over the entire surface of IPS beds shade out and prevent the growth of most weeds, making the IPS garden a snap to care for during the growing season. In addition, the leaves of mature plants touch one another, creating a miniature greenhouse under the leaves which keeps the temperature fairly constant, retains ground moisture longer, and keeps the soil loose and pliable. Conventional cultivating and mulching are therefore not necessary.

No Matter How Poor the Soil You Start With, . . .

Specially prepared soil really is the heart of all IPS gardens. And no matter what your soil is like right now, you can create an extremely fertile IPS garden with an easy, simple cultivation method that adds large amounts of conditioners and fertilizing ingredients to your present soil, changing its fertility, composition, and structure.

Ecologically Sound

IPS gardening is organic gardening. It maintains the ecological balance in your garden by using strictly organic materials to enhance soil fertility and natural methods to protect the garden from insects and diseases. Basically, these intensive organic methods create a vegetable garden that's vigorous and healthy and that generally becomes healthier and more fertile each and every gardening year.

So if you have a space problem, if you're a first-time gardener, if you've tried before and failed, or if you'd just like to try a system that's easy and satisfying and produces tremendous results, then come on and give the IPS method a try. Before you can say brown thumb twice, or maybe three times, you'll be well on your way to becoming a veteran Intensive Postage Stamp gardener.

CHAPTER TWO

How to Plan Your IPS Garden

There are few things more fun than planning the garden that you're going to grow next season.

The best wintertime garden dreamers make up dozens of drawings of what their next garden is going to look like. I suggest that you do it too. After all, things always go better with a plan. A good plan keeps your mistakes to a minimum by giving you some idea in advance of where to put your garden, what to plant in it, how much space to allocate, and what shape it should have.

Where to Put Your Garden

Of course the first thing to do in planning your garden is to decide where to put it. Actually your plants don't really care where they grow so long as you give them a lot of tender loving care.

5

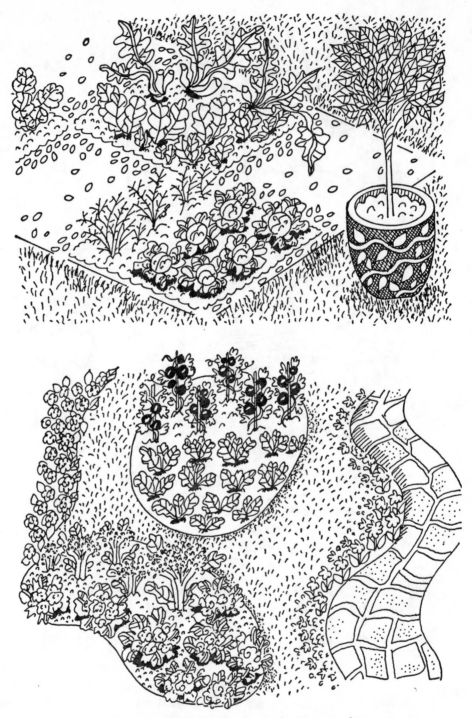

IPS gardens can be put anywhere and assume any shape.

To a vegetable, tender loving care is good fertile soil, enough water, and whatever heat and daylight it needs. In most cases, vegetables need direct sunlight, and you can satisfy this requirement practically anywhere. I have a bachelor friend who lives in one room behind a drugstore and grows a productive little garden in a sunny 5-by-9-foot space between the back door and a brick wall. By following a few rules you can certainly do as well in your own backyard. The main rule to consider is this: most vegetables need minimally about *six hours of direct sunlight.* If they get less, you're in trouble. So long as it receives this minimum amount of direct sunlight every day, you can put your garden almost anywhere. You can never give your vegetables too much sun.

There are a few other placement considerations.

Keep your garden bed at least twenty feet away from shallow-rooted trees like elms, maples, and poplars. Not only will the foliage of these trees block out the sun but their roots will also compete for water and nutrients. Generally, tree roots take food from the soil in a circle as far out as the tree's widest-reaching branches, and plants usually do poorly within this circle.

Don't put your garden in a depression that will collect standing water or near a downspout where the force from a sudden rain can wash out some of your plants.

Try to place your garden near a water outlet. This eliminates having to drag a hose long distances. Also try to place your garden as near the tool storage area as possible.

By proper placement of individual vegetables in your IPS garden you can produce extremely large quantities of vegetables in an extremely small space. The following are IPS planning rules that will help you obtain maximum results.

1. Plant tall vegetables on the north end of your garden to avoid shading the other vegetables, and plant the other vegetables in descending order of size down toward the south end of the garden.

2. Never mind about planting in rows. In an IPS garden you scatter your seeds to use all the space in your garden, and then thin out the seedlings (the small plants) as they come up. If you set out seedlings rather than seeds, space them without concern for straight rows. What you want is to have the mature plants just touch one another on all sides. (In Chapter 5 I'll discuss seeds and seedlings, as well as the best spacing for various plants.)

How to Design Your Garden

3. If your plot is large—say, 10 by 12 feet or 8 by 8 feet—you can plant your different types of vegetables in separate squares or rectangles. In large plots (more than 5 or 6 feet wide) you'll need pathways in order to reach all your plants. However, if the plot is narrow or small, simply block out irregular groups of vegetables and fill in the spaces any way you wish.

4. For root vegetables (such as carrots and beets), leafy vegetables (such as lettuce and spinach), and corn you need a little special planning. The areas chosen for each of these vegetables should be subdivided into thirds or fourths, and each subsection should be seeded or planted a week to ten days apart. In this way you get continual harvests: as one subsection finishes bearing mature vegetables, another begins. (You don't have this problem with plants like tomatoes and cucumbers, of course, which bear from the same plant over a long period of time.) After you've harvested a subsection of leafy or root vegetables, you can replant that subsection. That way you're making your garden produce everywhere all the time.

5. Use the air space above your garden as much as possible. Train tomatoes, cucumbers, and other vines and trailing plants up trellises, fences, poles, or whatnot, so that they won't be running all over your garden bed, crowding out the other plants. The better you get at this vertical growing, the more things you'll be able to pack into your IPS garden. (I'll give you several methods for doing this in the detailed sections on each vegetable, in Chapter 6.)

6. Don't limit yourself necessarily to vegetables. I always include marigolds and some herbs in my garden. You'll love the fragrance and color of a vegetable garden grown this way, . . . and, equally important, many veteran gardeners feel that herbs and some flowers have a tremendous beneficial effect on garden health. (We'll get to all this in Chapter 7.)

Garden Plans You Can Use

In the next few pages are various plans for some Intensive Postage Stamp gardens. The plans are intended as guidelines or possibilities only and should of course be modified by your own experience to fit your own needs. For one thing, you needn't limit yourself to conventional rectangles. Choose almost any shape for your garden that you wish—square, rectangular, triangular, circular, kidney-shaped, . . . you name it. Give vegetables water, sun, the right amount of heat, and good soil, and away they go. The shape of the garden generally doesn't mean a thing to them.

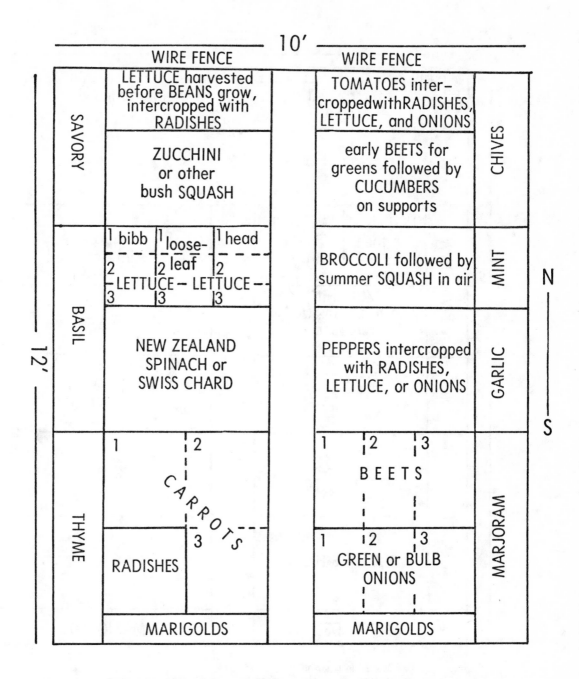

GARDEN 1. This plan illustrates some good IPS principles. Tall vine plants, such as tomatoes and beans, rise on the north end, and with these slow-growing vines are planted quick-maturing radishes, lettuce, and green onions. (The fences on which the vines grow can be made of chicken wire or any other convenient material.) Separate areas for carrots, beets, onions, and lettuce are divided into sections, to be planted one or two weeks apart.

9

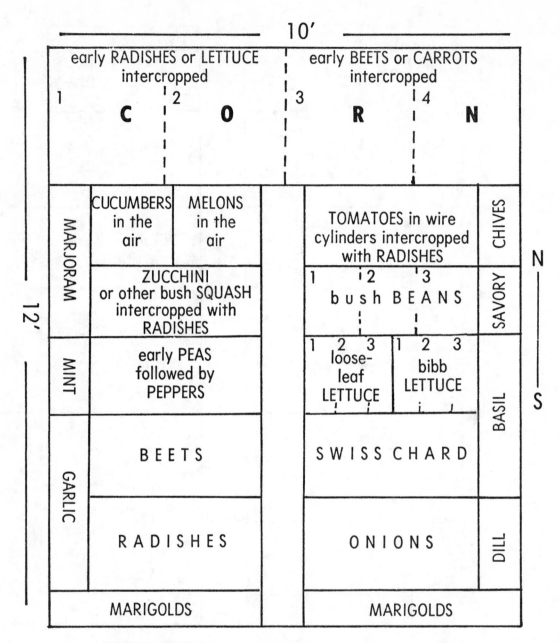

GARDEN 2. In this plan, corn is arranged in sections to be sown in successive weeks, and it is also planted in blocks, not single rows, to ensure cross-pollination (see page 64). Cucumbers and melons are trained in the air on posts or trellises, while tomatoes are grown within wire cylinders. Any of the areas assigned to root and leafy vegetables can be divided into sections, to be planted at one- or two-week intervals.

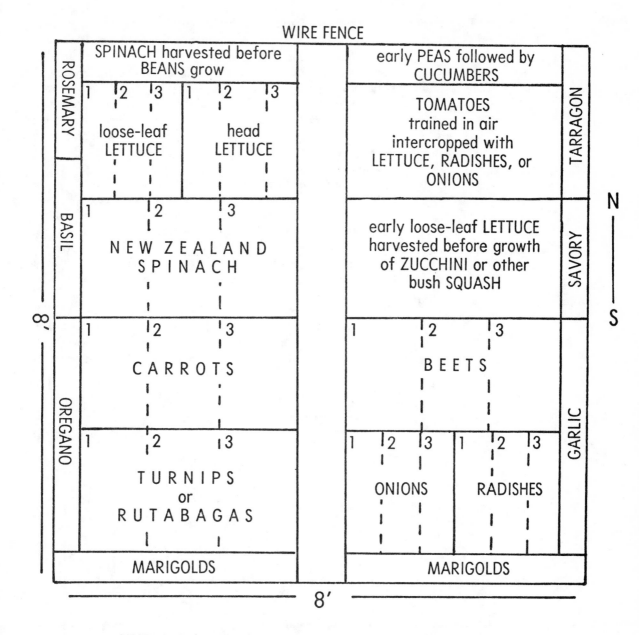

WIRE FENCE

| ROSEMARY | SPINACH harvested before BEANS grow | | early PEAS followed by CUCUMBERS | TARRAGON |

GARDEN 3. Cool weather plants, such as spinach and peas in this plan, can be planted early in spring and harvested before such warm weather plants as beans and cucumbers take over the same space. As in other plans, marigolds and herbs here form a border of companion plants (see Chapter 7), useful for their good effects on garden chemistry as well as for their appearance and aroma.

The Regular Flowerbed Garden

Who says that you have to grow a formal vegetable garden? Nobody, right? Not only can you mix vegetables with flowers in any flower bed, but a lot of gardeners will tell you that flower beds are really the natural place to grow vegetables. A friend of mine who follows this theory produces great quantities of vegetables. Her showy cabbage grows by itself, in a conspicuous spot. A number of vegetables make up the flower bed borders. Corn grows in the corner in one big bunch. Vine plants grow up the back fences. It's all very attractive and amusing.

Here are some rules that she gave me which I think you'll find helpful in "vegetablizing" your own flower beds:

1. Plant vines such as cucumbers and small melons against the walls. Plant beanstalks against a wall or stake them up. Plantings like this give your garden an especially lush look.

2. Use lettuce (especially leaf lettuce) and Swiss chard as a flower bed edging. Grow head lettuce just back of this.

3. Plant root crops in small sections.

4. Plant cabbage where you're looking for a show-off.

5. Plant corn in a good sunny corner. A 4-by-6 plot with plants 8 inches apart will turn out approximately ten ears.

6. Use peppers as an ornamental where they complement your other plants.

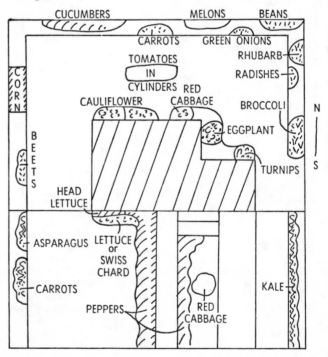

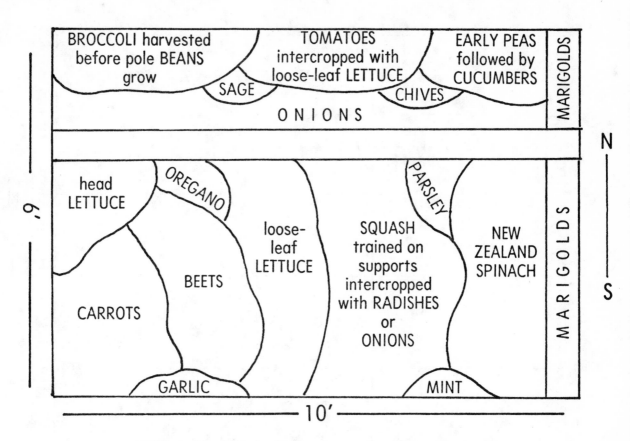

GARDEN 4. This small bed, a favorite of IPS gardeners, has curving plantings much like irregular, natural-looking flower beds. Groups of vegetables are arranged in waving patterns, and niches here and there are filled in with herbs.

FLOWER BED GARDEN. The house, in the center, with its walkway and driveway to the front, is surrounded by vegetables intermixed with borders of flowers and shrubbery. Many vegetable plants, such as peppers, kale, and cabbage, are very ornamental and make an attractive showing along with ornamental gardens or lawns.

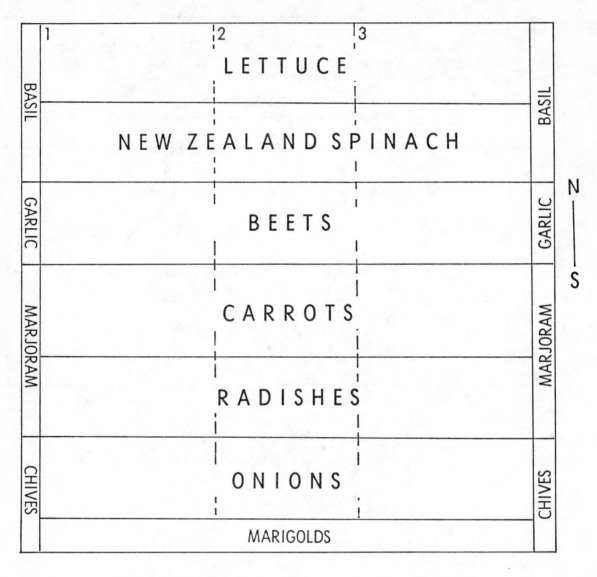

GARDEN 5. This plan is for the salad lover or for anyone who wants the easy-to-grow basics. The sections are planted successively, at one- or two-week intervals; and as soon as a section is harvested, it is replanted. Hence the continuous vegetable garden.

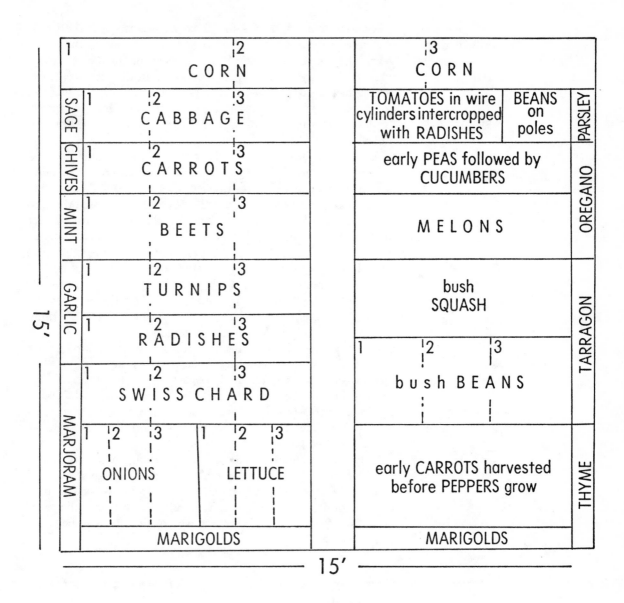

GARDEN 6. Here is the family food basket, large enough for a family of four (and some neighbors as well) and filled with most of the basic vegetables that anyone could want. It is also a continuous garden. Sections are planted in successive weeks, and new seeds or seedlings are sown whenever spaces are harvested and become vacant.

4-by-4
Boxed Gardens

For some reason, 4-by-4-foot boxed gardens spark the imagination of a lot of people, and I see more of them around every year. They're so neat and clean and easy to handle. You can walk all the way around them; you can thin the plants without having to get dirty; and you can have as many as you want in any arrangement you like—one or two or a bunch or whatever. I've gardened this way for several years now. I love and recommend it.

Actually a boxed garden is not really a "box," with a bottom. It's more of a frame. To make one, all you have to do is measure out a 4-by-4-foot space, prepare the soil, and then frame the space with standard 2-by-4 planks set slightly into the soil to hold in place. You can nail the corners for greater security if you wish. a 4-by-4 box like this is so much easier to handle that it appeals to my sense of energy conservation. I don't enjoy the gigantic task of putting together a big garden all at once; yet I can spade up a 4-by-4 bed, put a frame around it, and plant it in about half an hour. Then, over the next several weeks, I'll make up my entire garden one 4-by-4 bed at a time.

Generally I plant one or two vegetables per bed, with corn planted in three separate beds about two weeks apart. I split most beds in two, planting a different vegetable in each section—half to spinach, half to carrots, or whatever. These sections I also subdivide into thirds and plant two weeks apart. I plant all root and leafy vegetables this way. I train cucumbers, cantaloupe, beans, and other vines and trailers up stakes or trellises (see Chapter 6).

Now that we've explored some of the things that you should consider in planning the layout of your IPS garden, we can now turn to the soil itself—what it's like and how we can turn it into good fertile earth that will turn out an abundance of growing vegetables. These things we consider in the next two chapters.

PEAS followed by
pole BEANS
intercropped with
RADISHES

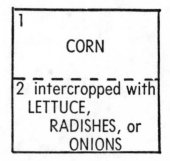

1

CORN

2 intercropped with
LETTUCE,
RADISHES, or
ONIONS

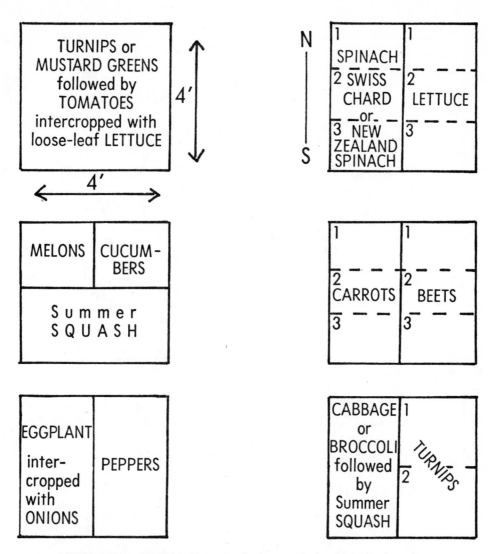

FOUR-BY-FOUR BOXED GARDEN. Small plots, each four feet by four feet, framed in by wooden planks, make neat arrangements and ones easily prepared and cared for. They are flexible and avoid the fuss of having to set plants north or south and having to arrange companionable plants in set patterns. They are also convenient for the gardener who has only small isolated patches of usable ground in his yard.

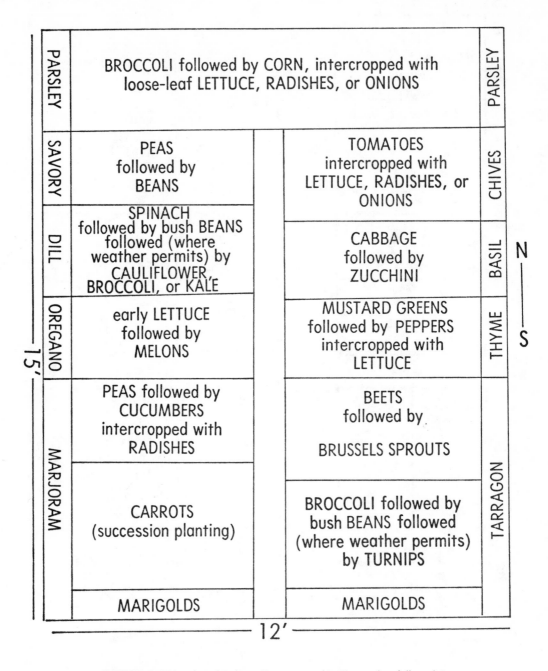

PARSLEY	BROCCOLI followed by CORN, intercropped with loose-leaf LETTUCE, RADISHES, or ONIONS		PARSLEY
SAVORY	PEAS followed by BEANS	TOMATOES intercropped with LETTUCE, RADISHES, or ONIONS	CHIVES
DILL	SPINACH followed by bush BEANS followed (where weather permits) by CAULIFLOWER, BROCCOLI, or KALE	CABBAGE followed by ZUCCHINI	BASIL
OREGANO	early LETTUCE followed by MELONS	MUSTARD GREENS followed by PEPPERS intercropped with LETTUCE	THYME
MARJORAM	PEAS followed by CUCUMBERS intercropped with RADISHES	BEETS followed by BRUSSELS SPROUTS	TARRAGON
	CARROTS (succession planting)	BROCCOLI followed by bush BEANS followed (where weather permits) by TURNIPS	
	MARIGOLDS	MARIGOLDS	

15'

12'

N — S

GARDEN 7. This plan develops "crop stretching" to the full, relying on succession planting, intercropping, and catch cropping (see pages 45-46). In this plan, as well as in others, the herbs and marigolds, though useful, are not essential; the areas for vegetables can instead be expanded to assume all the garden space.

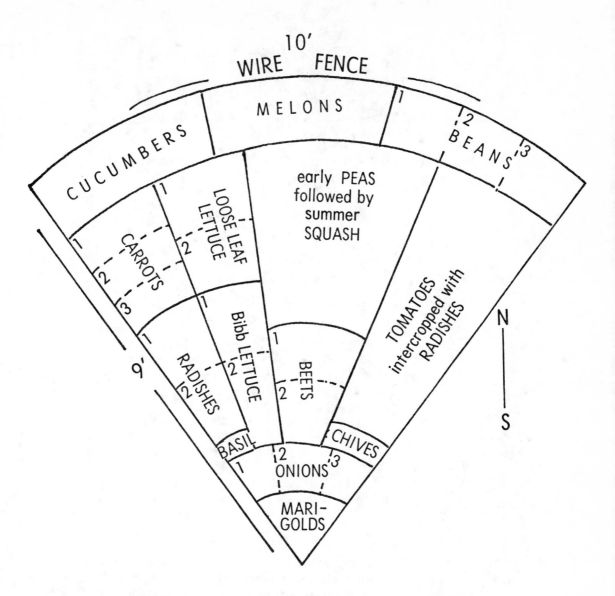

GARDEN 8. A vegetable garden can take any shape, so long as tall plants are set to the north and small ones to the south. Favorite vegetables—not necessarily those shown in this plan—can be planted wherever space is available, in triangles, circles, wedges, or rectangles.

CHAPTER THREE

What Goes into Your Soil

Put yourself in this picture. It's a beautiful day. There's not a cloud in the sky. The temperature's in the middle 80s. And there you are in your backyard picking loads of vegetables from your own small garden tucked away in the corner of your property—tomatoes, peas, onions, corn. . . . You've grown them all. More than you ever dreamed possible from such a small space.

Impossible?

Of course not.

After all, that's exactly what an Intensive Postage Stamp garden is intended to do and is exactly what you're going to learn how to do in the next few chapters.

The condition of the soil, which we'll be discussing, can actually make or break the productiveness of our garden. It is, in effect, the motor; and if we expect to grow a lot of vegetables in a small space (as we do), it's extremely important to build the very best soil-motor possible.

Look at it this way. Suppose you buy a Lincoln Continental, and after you get it home you remove its engine and install a Volkswagen motor. Then you start on a trip. You wouldn't expect to rip up the road getting to your destination, because you know that a Volkswagen engine can't handle a Lincoln Continental.

But suppose instead of replacing the Continental engine with a Volkswagen motor you simply leave the original engine in place and take off on your trip. Now, if you want to, you can beat most of the cars on the road.

Now, imagine that you take the Continental engine out again, and this time (providing you can figure out a way to do it) you put the engine in a Volkswagen body. Now you can beat anything in sight . . . and then some.

That's something like what we're trying to do. We want to squeeze every last bit of productivity out of the soil in our IPS garden. What we'll do in effect is to install a Lincoln engine in a Volkswagen body. We're going to make the soil in your garden superproductive.

I know a gardener (maybe I should say a would-be gardener) who simply goes out in her backyard, lightly tills the soil, drops in some seed, waters, and calls it a day. She doesn't bother to improve the soil structure or make sure that it contains the proper nutrients. She thereafter fails to water regularly or care much about nurturing her plants at all. What she does do is produce the lousiest-looking vegetables that you've ever seen. She claims that mother nature hates her, and she may just be right.

Naturally we'd all like to pop seeds in the ground and have the garden automatically crank out carloads of super vegetables. But unfortunately it doesn't work like that.

There is a way out, however, for if you'll take the time in the beginning to build your soil right, your IPS garden will reward you (from then on) with some of the greatest vegetables that you've ever seen. Now, as a starter, let's take a peek at what's under the ground in your backyard.

How Soil Works

All that most people see when they look at their soil is a bunch of dirt. It's the stuff that comes in on the kids clothes, . . . that has to be swept off the back porch, . . . or that has to be cleaned up off the kitchen floor. Actually, however, soil is a lot more than that.

Every square foot of soil swarms with millions of bacteria and other microorganisms. Potentially the organic material that's in the soil or the raw material that you deposit there—leaves, grass clippings, garbage, and so forth—contains essential elements that plants can use in their own growth. Unfortunately, these elements are tied up in such a way that our vegetables can't touch them. Fortunately for our plants, the soil bacteria rip into the dead material in the soil, breaking it down and converting it into forms that plants can gobble up and build with.

How fast the soil bacteria act on this raw material depends on the nature of the material itself, the temperature, the amount of air available, and the soil moisture. In the spring, when the soil warms up, the numbers of bacteria in the soil and the bacterial action increase tremendously. When you add fresh organic material, the bacteria immediately attack it, breaking it down into food for your plants. The bacterial organisms themselves need nitrogen to take care of their growing needs. And if you don't have nitrogen in the material that you put in the garden, the bacteria will end up stealing it from the vegetables you're trying to grow. That's something that you don't want to see happen.

You get around this problem by building a compost pile for organic material. This pile lets the initial bacterial decomposition take place outside your soil. Then when you turn this material into your soil, the nutrients are in a form that plants can use immediately. (We'll get to this shortly.)

How Soil Is Structured

Basically, there are three kinds of soil: clay, sand, and loam. Clay soil has particles so small that you can't see them without help. They are extremely close together and take in water slowly. Once the clay particles absorb water, they hold it so tightly that it's almost impossible for plants to utilize it; and air can't get in. When clay dries, it's even worse. Plant roots have difficulty penetrating, and the soil itself contains little air and water.

Sand, on the other hand, has particles many times larger than clay. Air penetrates deeply, and water moves through it too rapidly, dissolving away many of the nutrients.

Loam is somewhere between these two extremes. Loam has clay, sand, and a good supply of decomposed organic material called humus. The grains have good structure. The soil drains well, yet retains enough water for plant growth. Air can circulate, and the soil provides plenty of room for roots to grow easily.

Don't worry if your backyard isn't loam. As I mentioned in Chapter 1, in an IPS garden we completely renovate the soil so that it doesn't really matter what kind of soil you start with.

I might also mention here a thing that some gardeners seem to worry about a great deal: the pH of their soil. This is the measure of whether your soil is sweet (alkaline) or sour (acid). The pH scale runs from 0 for extremely acid to 7 for neutral, to 14 for extremely alkaline. Most vegetables prefer soils that are neutral or slightly acid, that is, with a *p*H of 6.5 to 7.0. There's no doubt that *p*H is important. Generally, however, when we make up our IPS beds, we automatically make them just about right for vegetables. Unless you've got a really unusual problem, like trying to garden near alkali flats or salt marshes (alkaline soil) or in a peat bog (acid soil), just forget about the *p*H problem and simply make up your garden according to the instructions given in this book. If you do have one of those freak problems, contact your local nurseryman and ask how other gardeners in the area have handled it. Once you've solved this, then you can proceed to make up your IPS garden in the regular manner.

Getting the Ingredients for your IPS Garden Soil

I don't have to tell you that plants need to eat just like you do. Now, that's not technically correct, of course, but everybody knows that plants need certain soil conditions and certain nutrients—sixteen of them—in order to be healthy and vigorous. There are three major nutrients—nitrogen (N), phosphorus (P), and potassium (K)—and a number of minor and trace elements, including calcium, zinc, iron, manganese, copper, sulfur, magnesium, and a few others.

You'd be surprised at what an effect these have. When I was a graduate student I worked in the college greenhouse, where one of my professors grew tomatoes in chemical solutions in jars. Some jars contained all the nutrients that the plants needed, and they looked great; others had one nutrient missing from each jar. You could really tell the difference. In some jars whole leaves turned yellow. In others the yellow crept along the veins or did something similar. Generally those plants needed every single one of those elements to stay really happy.

To provide these nutrients in our IPS gardens, we add four organic ingredients: compost, manure, bone meal, and wood ash (or some substitutes). Sometimes we add a fifth ingredient, fish emulsion. In the remainder of this chapter we will take a closer look at each of these ingredients, because they are what make our Intensive Postage Stamp gardens thrive. In the next chapter, I'll show you what we do with these ingredients once we have them.

Compost—and a Temporary Substitute

Probably the most important ingredient that you'll add to your IPS bed is compost—the mixture of decayed leaves, grass clippings, garbage, and other organic matter that you prepare yourself in piles and then add to the soil. In composting, the organic matter is broken down by bacterial action into food that your vegetable plants can use immediately. Without it (or some good substitute), you'll get only so-so vegetables. With it, the ground seems to come alive. Also it helps marvelously to give the soil a lighter texture, letting the soil breathe.

You can prepare compost very easily. Detailed instructions for different types of composting are given in the appendix. Most composting, though, takes time. It can take a few weeks or even a few months for the raw organic material in a compost pile to break down into compounds that vegetable plants can use. For this reason you should begin as soon as possible to build your compost piles for your garden.

In the meantime, don't let a lack of compost stop you from preparing an IPS garden. Simply substitute rotted manure (see below) whenever we call for compost.

Animal Manures

We really need animal manures in our garden, for they add many needed nutrients, especially nitrogen. But just to make the choice a little harder for us, every one of them has different properties and varying amounts of nitrogen, phosphorus, and potassium.

Generally, you should use rotted manure, not fresh. The bacteria in your soil will need extra nitrogen to break down fresh manure, and this can divert some of the nitrogen from your plants. Moreover—like organic materials that have been composted—manure that has already rotted or decomposed is in a form that your plants can use more easily. You can obtain rotted manure by placing fresh manure in a pile, covering it with a thin layer of dirt, and letting it stand a few months. If a pile (even a tiny pile) of manure in your backyard doesn't appeal to you, try acquiring it, as I do, from a nearby stable. In January the stable owner puts the fresh manure in a big pile and covers it with dirt to eliminate the smell. When I haul my manure away in March, it's in just the right shape.

Dried manure, which you can buy from a nursery, is also usually just right, and it can be worked into your garden soil directly from the sack.

Do not buy steer manure, however, because its high salt content offsets any benefit that the manure might have. Although these salts can be leached out by watering the steer manure, this leaching also washes out the nitrogen.

Hen, horse, sheep, and rabbit manures are known as "hot" manures because of their high nitrogen content. Cow and hog manures are called "cold" manures because they are fairly wet, are low in nitrogen, and break down fairly slowly. I prefer using horse manure, for I think it gives me the best results.

I suggest that you start out using whatever you find available (given the cautions above) and then later experiment to see which gives you the best results in your particular garden.

Bone Meal and Another Phosphorus Material

Generally we supply phosphorus (one of the major nutrients) to our plants by adding bone meal. Bone meal has a whopping amount of phosphoric acid—20 to 25 percent or more—as well as 1 to 2 percent nitrogen; and vegetables love it. You can buy steamed bone meal at hardware stores, nurseries, or wherever garden products are sold.

If you like, you can substitute rock phosphate or superphosphate for bone meal. This is a finely ground rock powder, containing up to 30 percent phosphoric acid.

Wood Ash and Other Potassium Materials

Wood ash supplies the potassium needed by your plants. Most wood ash contains 7 to 8 percent potassium and can be obtained simply by burning wood outdoors or in your fireplace. (Wood ashes should not be allowed to stand in the rain, because most of the potassium will be leached away.)

If you have trouble getting wood ash, it's possible to substitute greensand or granite dust, which you can buy at many nurseries. Both of these materials contain about 6 to 8 percent potassium. Both also contain a number of minor and trace mineral nutrients.

Fish Emulsion and Other Fertilizers

Fish emulsion generally has 5 to 10 percent nitrogen and sometimes phosphorus and potassium, although many brands are marked on the bottle 5-0-0, which, in nursery language, means respectively 5 percent nitrogen, no phosphorus, and no potassium. I use fish emulsion in an IPS garden during midseason simply to add nitrogen to those plants that are pretty heavy feeders. I'll discuss how much you need and when in Chapter 6, in treating individual vegetables.

Some gardeners prefer to use liquid seaweed in place of fish emulsion. It contains nitrogen, phosphorus, and a number of minerals.

There are other materials containing nitrogen that you can add to your IPS garden. Blood meal, which you can buy at most nurseries, contains up to 15 percent nitrogen and usually some phosphorous and potassium. Activated sewerage sludge (Milorganite) contains up to 6 percent nitrogen and is processed and sold by a number of cities. Cottonseed meal contains about 7 percent nitrogen.

Any of these fertilizers can be added to your soil to give your feeding plants an extra boost. Avoid, however, all chemical fertilizers.

The Earthworm   Earthworms, like bacteria, are great for the soil and will be extremely helpful in keeping your IPS bed in shape. By burrowing, feeding, and excreting, earthworms let air and moisture in and break up the soil particles. They usually don't go very deep, but the minute that plant roots start going down, earthworms go with them, making the soil better.

The gray pink ones (*Helodrilus caliginosus* and *Helodrilus trapezoides*) are important to your garden. The red one (*Eisenia foetida*), the fishworm, is not so good since he wants to fool around in damp spongy places instead of getting down to work in garden soils. You'll find him great in compost piles, however, and later you may want to buy a few to add when you make your own compost. (Fishworms can be ordered from W. Atlee Burpee Company; see appendix.)

The earthworm improves the soil by swallowing it and later expelling it in the form of castings. What actually happens is that the earthworm takes in the soil, grinds it up, mixes it with calcium carbonate, pulverizes it, sends it on through the intestine to be digested by enzymes, and them excretes it. These final earthworm castings contain nitrogen, phosphorus, and potassium, all elements that our vegetables need. And when the earthworm dies, his body adds a good nitrogen fertilizer to the soil.

It is important to note here that chemicals and earthworms just don't mix, at least not well. Chemical fertilizers seem to decrease the number of earthworms in the soil, killing them or driving them off; ammonium sulfate is particularly harmful. Many insect sprays also are toxic to earthworms and will cause the population in the soil to dwindle.

Earthworms actually are a little finicky about the soil in general. You can't put them in infertile or hard, clayey soils and expect good results. They like rich soil; and if they don't have it, they just take off.

Earthworms make a good soil even better. So, when possible, dig up earthworms from other parts of the yard (or anywhere else) and deposit them in your future vegetable garden. You'll just have to search around by turning dirt over with a shovel until you find them, but generally there are lots of them in most flower beds.

That takes care of the preparation of your soil. Remember that creating the proper kind of soil bristling with the right organic nutrients is the most important thing that you can do in your garden. And your vegetables will love you for it. In the next chapter I'll show you how to put all these nutrients into your garden.

CHAPTER FOUR

How to Get Your Soil Ready

In vegetable gardening there's nothing at all that's difficult or very much work, at least not on the scale that we're doing it. Getting the soil ready in the first place will take more effort than anything else you'll do.

Actually, IPS gardening is different. In a conventional garden you have to dig up the soil in the first place and then, throughout the season, cultivate and weed. A heck of a lot of work. But in an IPS garden you can generally forget this. Digging up the ground initially is the big push, but a fairly easy one. After that, except for watering, you can more or less coast. And, believe me, that's the kind of gardening I really like.

As I mentioned in Chapter 3, the whole idea in the IPS garden is to create a superfertile, well-textured soil that will support the growth of a large quantity of vegetables in a small

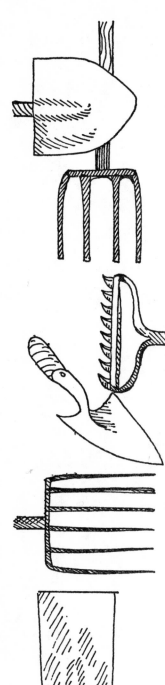

space. For ways of preparing the soil you have a choice. You can use what I call the general intensive method or the modified French Intensive methods.

With the general intensive method you can plow a small bed in about ten minutes using a rotary tiller or Rototiller (that's a power cultivator with rotating blades that tear up the soil). After that, it's simple to spade in your compost, manure, and other nutrients and rake over the soil. The Rototiller method is easy and can produce good results. It has only one general drawback. Because the Rototiller breaks down everything in the soil to about the same consistency, it does tend to destroy some of the soil structure and the layering effect that help to create soil fertility.

The modified French Intensive methods, on the other hand, employ hand tools only, such as a spade and a rake; and these methods structure the soil in a special way.

While we're on the subject of tools, I should emphasize that you won't need fancy tools to build your IPS beds unless you intend to use a rotary tiller. In that case, you'll need to borrow, buy, or rent one. Most equipment rental agencies, many hardware stores, and some garden centers have them available. (Consult the Yellow Pages of your telephone directory, under Rental Service Stores & Yards or under Garden & Lawn Equipment & Supplies. Such stores as Sears and Montgomery Ward sell rotary tillers under such names as Roto-Spaders and Tillers.)

You can make up most beds with a round-point shovel (that's the common ordinary long-handled one). It lets you turn dirt easily because the blade attaches at a slight angle from the handle.

If you have a lot of rocks or tough soil, a four-pronged garden fork will let you dig up soils that you can't penetrate easily with a shovel.

To work in compost, bone meal, and other ingredients, a spade, with its flat blade, is extremely useful.

To move partially decomposed compost, straw, and leaves, you'll need a manure fork. This lets you pick up large quantities of materials easily.

A rake helps in leveling beds and breaking up clods. A hoe can handle most other garden chores.

You will also need a small garden trowel for planting seedlings or roots and doing other kinds of small digging.

In all cases I recommend that you not buy the cheapest tools on the market. They'll bend or break easily and cost you more in replacements in the long run. Invest in good sturdy tools.

Rototilling the Soil

Adding Compost

Spading in

Adding the rest

Raking Smooth

I usually dig my IPS beds with a spade or shovel, and it takes me a while; but one of my friends who stands 5-feet-2-inches tall and weighs 96 pounds puts hers together quickly and easily with a Rototiller. It's that simple. If you intend to garden in an area where the soil is hard and clayey and difficult to spade, it may be an especially good idea to rototill the first year. In subsequent years the soil will be looser, and you needn't rely on rototilling. In any case, here is the procedure:

1. Rototill your bed at least one foot deep.

2. If you have clayey soil, use a spade or spading fork to turn sand and compost into soil until your bed consists of ⅓ compost, ⅓ sand, and ⅓ original soil. For sandy soils, turn compost into your bed until you have ⅓ to ½ compost, the rest original soil. For in-between soils just estimate how much you'll need of one thing or another in order to wind up with a mixture that contains at least ⅓ compost, that is loose and fairly fine, and that has good air space and is easy to work. While you're preparing your soil, you'll want to remove all the rocks you find. (Sand, by the way, can be purchased from most building supply centers or garden centers. Or you can haul it from the beds or shores of rivers or freshwater lakes or even from sand dunes near seashores if the dunes are not touched by the sea and if rains have leached out all the salt.)

3. Level the bed with a rake.

4. Over the entire bed spread a 2-inch layer of rotted manure, a sprinkling of bone meal (4 pounds per 50 square feet), and a small dose of wood ash (3 pounds per 50 square feet)—or any of the substitutes given in Chapter 3. Using a rake, turn this into just the top portion of the soil, and then rake the topsoil to a light texture.

Modified French Intensive Methods

The modified French Intensive methods that follow are good ways to achieve superfertilization because they allow you to control soil texture. They help put the soil in condition so that water can come up automatically from below and so that gases produced by bacterial action can come up from the roots and air can go down and thus make the soil breathe.

You can start the soil breathing by simply opening it with a shovel or spade. But to achieve good water conduction you want the soil generally coarse below and fine-textured above. The moment that you get dirt clods in the surface soil or fine grains below you interfere with water conduction.

General Hand Method

In the general hand method, you achieve a partial layering of nutrients and get a very fertile topsoil and loose subsoil. Here's how it goes:

1. For heavy clay soils, cover the entire bed 6 to 8 inches with a mixture of ½ compost, and ½ sand. For sandy soils you instead cover the bed 4 to 5 inches with pure compost. You primarily want to wind up with a soil composition of ⅓ compost, ⅓ sand, and ⅓ other soil ingredients. Therefore, adjust your addition of compost and sand to meet the needs of your own soil, whether clayey or sandy or something in-between. Just estimate. The main idea is to come out with the soil mixture that contains at least ⅓ compost, that is loose and fairly fine, and that has good air space and is easy to work. (While you're preparing your soil, you should take out all rocks.)

2. Start at one side of the bed and dig a trench along the entire side. Make the trench one spade wide and deep—that is,

REMOVING TOPSOIL FROM FIRST TRENCH | SPADING SUBSOIL IN FIRST TRENCH | FILLING UP FIRST TRENCH

about 9 to 10 inches deep. Put the excavated topsoil (along with the compost-sand mix) aside where you can get it later.

3. Loosen the subsoil in the trench that you've just created one spade depth more—to about 18 to 20 inches below the original surface. Make sure that this subsoil is nice and loose but not too fine. You want the soil to grade from a fairly coarse texture at the bottom to a fairly fine texture at the top.

4. Remove one spade depth of topsoil (including the compost-sand mix) from the strip of bed directly beside the trench that you've just opened, and fill in your trench. Make sure that you mix the topsoil and compost-sand mixture well in the trench that you're now filling up.

5. You now have a new trench next to the original one that you just filled up. As before, loosen the subsoil in this trench and then fill the trench with the topsoil (and compost-sand mix) from the adjacent strip.

6. Now, in the same manner, dig one trench after the other across the width of your bed until you've finished the entire bed. After you've worked trench by trench and reached the very last row of your garden, take the topsoil with the compost-sand mixture that you laid aside originally from the first trench and fill in the last trench.

7. Let the soil surface stay rough a few days so that air can get into the soil. Then, using a spade and a rake, work the topsoil to a fine texture. Make sure that you break up all clods.

8. Over the entire surface spread about 2 inches of rotted manure, a small amount of bone meal (4 pounds per 50 square feet), and a small amount of wood ash (3 pounds per 50 square feet)—or any substitute given in Chapter 3. Work these materials into the top 5 or 6 inches of topsoil, and rake smooth.

SPADING SUBSOIL IN SECOND TRENCH | FILLING IN SECOND TRENCH | FILLING IN LAST TRENCH / FINAL

Because you've added extra material to your bed you'll end up with a slight mound. You'll also have a soil that's rich in nutrients, takes in air easily, lets fertile gases come up, and drains perfectly.

The Expert Method

The expert method is similar to the previous modified French Intensive Method, except that the various ingredients are added at certain depths in the soil. The reason for this more precise layering is that plants seems to grow towards food they like. Cantaloupe roots, for instance, will race straight toward a pile of manure seven to fifteen feet away. Similarly, every plant root seems to know exactly what's going on below and will grow a lot faster to get there to the right nutrients. The plant root also seems to like different kinds of nutrients at different depths. It's almost as if plants want variety, and when they find something different they say, . . . breakfast, oh boy! . . . lunch, wow! . . . dinner, great! When the layering is done right, root growth speeds up.

With the expert method the bed is made up in two stages. In the first stage the bed is dug up, sand is added to the soil, and then the bed is left rough for a few days. In the second stage, occurring several days later, all other ingredients—compost and other materials—are added to the soil. Now let's take a look at the individual steps.

1. For clayey soils, cover the entire bed 2 to 3 inches deep with sand. Adjust the amount of sand to meet the needs of your own soil, whether clayey, sandy, or something in-between. When this stage is finished you want to come out roughly with soil that is ½ sand, ½ original soil.

2. Start at one side of the bed and dig a trench along the entire side. Make the trench one spade wide and deep— that is, about 9 to 10 inches deep. Put the excavated topsoil (along with the sand) aside where you can get it later.

3. Loosen the subsoil in the trench that you've just created one spade depth more—to about 18 to 20 inches below the original surface. Make sure that this subsoil is nice and loose but not too fine. As I said before, you want the soil to grade from a fairly coarse texture at the bottom to a fairly fine texture at the top.

4. Remove one spade depth of topsoil (including the sand) from the strip of bed directly beside the trench that you've just opened, and fill in your trench. Make sure that you mix the sand and soil well in the trench that you're now filling up.

5. You now have a new trench next to the first one that you filled up. In this new trench loosen the subsoil in the same manner as before. Again, fill in the trench with topsoil (and sand) from the adjacent strip.

6. Dig one trench after another across the width of the bed, always loosening the subsoil and mixing the topsoil and sand, until you've finished the entire bed. Into the very last trench put the topsoil (and sand) that you laid aside originally from the first trench.

7. Leave the garden rough for a few days.

8. Now go back and excavate the topsoil from each strip again, one by one. As you then return the topsoil to each trench, you add different nutrients at different levels. First, spread a small amount of bone meal (4 pounds per 50 square feet) at the bottom of the topsoil. Add some topsoil. Second, spread a 4-inch layer of compost. Add some more topsoil. Third, add about 2 inches of rotted manure. Add some more topsoil. Fourth, add a small amout of wood ash (3 pounds per 50 square feet). Spread over the remaining topsoil. (Use the substitute nutrients cited in Chapter 3, if you wish.)

9. Rake the soil at the top (don't disturb the strata) until it has a very fine texture.

This method also gives you a slight mound. It generally produces the best results because it stimulates root growth by providing different nutrients at different levels. It also takes more work.

Variations on the Intensive Methods

There are a number of variations possible with all the intensive methods. Here are a couple that you might want to try:

Some gardeners simply like to dump all the ingredients together into the finished or ripe compost so they don't have to work with the fertilizing ingredients separately. Simply add one part rotted manure for every two parts of ripe compost. Add one cup of bone meal and one cup of wood ash (or their substitutes) for each cubic foot of compost. Work the mixture into the bed all together.

If you don't have compost yet—and you probably won't, if you're a beginning gardener—you can start your garden using rotted manure. Simply substitute manure for compost.

Putting Moisture into the Soil

After you've dug up the soil and added the nutrients, you can begin planting any time. You should, however, deeply soak the soil with water a day or two *before* you actually sow your seeds or set out your seedlings. If it hasn't rained recently, you may have to water for a long while in order to get moisture down to a depth of at least 10 inches.

Refeeding

In the course of a growing season, every time you take out a crop you're going to have to refeed the soil before planting anything new. It's no big deal. To revitalize the soil, simply spread a couple of inches of rotted manure and a couple of inches of compost on top of the garden bed and work it in as thoroughly as possible. Because you really worked up the bed the first time, you won't have much trouble now. Also add small amounts of bone meal and wood ash (or substitutes)—4 pounds of bone meal per 50 square feet and 3 pounds of wood ash per 50 square feet.

Every new year in the spring, of course, you should completely spade or rototill your beds again, according to the intensive methods described in this chapter.

Crop Rotation

In addition to adding compost and other ingredients each growing season, you should rotate the crops to keep the soil healthy.

Some vegetables make heavy demands on the soil (heavy feeders); others take out very little (light feeders); and a few (the legumes) restore soil fertility. By moving these various kinds of vegetables around in our IPS beds we can keep our soil in good shape throughout the years and even add vigor to it as we go along.

Heavy feeders should be followed when possible by legumes (beans and peas), which restore the soil fertility. After the legumes, you then plant the light feeders. In an IPS garden this rotation is a little difficult because we try to plant taller vegetables to the north and the smaller ones to the south. But if you want to give the soil a break, you must restore the balance whenever possible.

In sum, as you continue gardening the IPS way, your soil—if you treat it right—will just keep getting better and better. If there's any secret to turning brown thumbs into bright green ones that grow big bunches of vegetables in a very small space, the IPS way is it. Once you've created the right soil conditions in the first place and keep adding compost and other nutrients each growing season, you'll wind up with a soil that will continually grow vigorous, healthy vegetables from then on with only a minimum of additional effort.

Light Feeders

beets — carrots — onions
radishes — rutabagas
turnips

Heavy Feeders

broccoli — Brussels sprouts
cabbage — cauliflower
corn — cucumbers
eggplant — kale — lettuce
melons — mustard greens
New Zealand spinach
okra — peppers — spinach
squash — Swiss chard
tomatoes

Soil Restorers

beans — peas

CHAPTER FIVE

When and How to Plant

Just how do you know when to plant so that everything comes up rapidly and keeps right on going to maturity?

That's a good question, . . . and there are good answers.

I really become frustrated when I turn a seed package over to read the planting instructions and they merely say, "Plant after all danger of frost has passed." Unfortunately, although this advice is good as far as it goes, it is inadequate because different classes of vegetables need different amounts of growing heat. Let's begin by looking at the question of cool and warm seasons.

Mother Nature's Time Clock

Vegetables are divided basically into warm season and cool season crops.

Generally, plants that we harvest for their fruit (the part of the plant in which seeds are produced)—such as tomatoes, squash, peppers, eggplant, melons, and lima bans—need a lot of heat and long days to grow well and form fruit. You might be safe from any more frost; but if there isn't enough heat during the day to satisfy a plant's heat requirements, it will just sit there and do nothing. I've planted tomatoes in April, for instance, and wondered why they weren't growing. Then suddenly the days started to turn warm and the plants took off. Since then, I've experimented with planting tomatoes at one week intervals starting in March. My early plants never seem to reach maturity any faster than the plants set out later because their development is held back by cool weather.

Cool season plants, on the other hand, do quite well when the weather is on the cool side. These are generally the leafy and root vegetables: carrots, beets, spinach, cabbage, lettuce, and so on. You also have to include peas as a cool season plant even though you harvest the fruit. When the weather is cool and the days short, these plants put all their efforts into forming leafy or root materials, but when the days begin to warm up they stop producing leafy material and start to go to seed. As a result, you generally have to plant cool season vegetables early so that they can achieve the right size before the weather becomes too hot. You can also plant them late so that they mature in the cooler days of fall.

Besides warm season and cool season vegetables, we also have early and late varieties of most vegetables. The early varieties require less heat to mature than the late. If you want to start your vegetables early, you can start with one of the early varieties, then follow through with a later one for that particular type of vegetable (corn, for instance) all season long.

Or, if you live in an area that is continually cool throughout the summer, never rising above the 70s, you might plant only an early variety, because it requires less heat to mature than the late variety.

All of this means that you have to watch the heat requirements of particular plants to know when to plant in your area. Experienced gardeners get so that they know exactly when to plant for best results.

Fortunately for those of us with latent brown thumbs, nature provides a guide that we can use effectively to know when to plant. This guide relies on the blooming of fairly common plants, and since mother nature does all the juggling herself, the system is far more accurate than arbitrary planting rules or a good guess. Here's what to watch for:

Condition	Plant
Development of color in flowers from spring bulbs, such as tulips or narcissus	Plant beets, carrots, leaf lettuce, onions, peas, radishes, and spinach
Appearance of plum and cherry blossoms	Plant head lettuce
Appearance of apple, cherry, quince, and strawberry blossoms	Plant everything else cucumbers, melons, squash, tomatoes, and so on

The only problem in referring to a frost map is that it's impossible to group the entire country into clearly defined climatic regions. Within each region you'll find many different miniclimates where the average date of the last killing frost varies. Spring nighttime temperatures, for instance, are warmer near the ocean, cooler in inland valleys, and still cooler at higher elevations inland. Geographical points only a few miles apart may have radically different temperatures. This means that you can only generalize. A frost map can be helpful, however, in determining approximately when to plant in the spring.

To use the frost map, simply pick out your zone on the map to determine the average date of the last killing frost. The vegetable planting list in the right-hand margin will then tell you approximately on what date to plant particular vegetables. For instance, if you live in Zone 3, the average dates of the last killing frost fall between May 1 and May 15. Referring to the vegetable planting list, to the right, you will find that you can plant kale sometime between April 1 and April 15, carrots between May 1 and May 15, and tomatoes after May 15 when the ground has warmed up.

Planting with a Frost Map

1. In Zones 6, 7, 8, and 9, plant these vegetables from fall to early spring. In all other zones plant these vegetables 2 to 4 weeks before the last killing frost in spring.
   broccoli — Brussels sprouts kale — lettuce — mustard greens — onions — peas radishes — rutabagas turnips

2. Plant these vegetables on approximately the date of the last frost. They tolerate cool weather and very light frost.
   beets — cabbage — carrots cauliflower — Swiss chard

3. Plant these vegetables after the ground has warmed up.
   beans — corn — cucumbers eggplant — melons — okra peppers — squash tomatoes

Zone 1 — June 15
Zone 2 — May 15-31
Zone 3 — May 1-15
Zone 4 — April 15-30
Zone 5 — April 1-15
Zone 6 — March 15-31
Zone 7 — March 1-15
Zone 8 — Feb. 1-28
Zone 9 — Jan. 15-31
Zone 10 — Frost Free

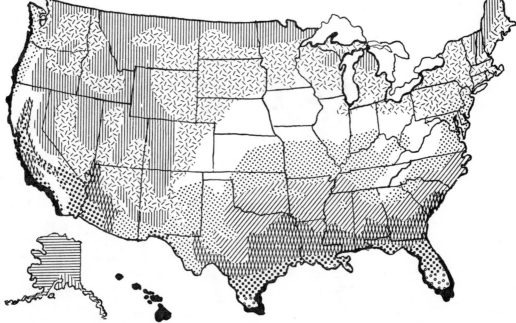

Planting by Moon Cycles

Planting by moon cycles sounds like an old wives tale, doesn't it? Yet we know, for instance, that both the moon and the sun affect the tides and that the pull is greater at certain times than at others. If you watch the growth of your garden awhile in relation to various phases of the moon, you'll see some startling things. There seem to be noticeable spurts of growth in the garden that coincide with the new moon and the full moon. Some gardeners swear by this and will plant only at times when they feel that the gravitational effect is best.

There's a little old lady who used to live across the street from my house who was from the hills of South Carolina and claimed that she could grow green things better than anybody else. Actually she did a pretty good job. She swore by moon cycles and wouldn't plant unless everything was right. At that time, I used to be skeptical about this, but she would have seeds sprouting up in four or five days when it took me two weeks or longer. Now, for anybody who'd like to give a try, I'll give you her rules.

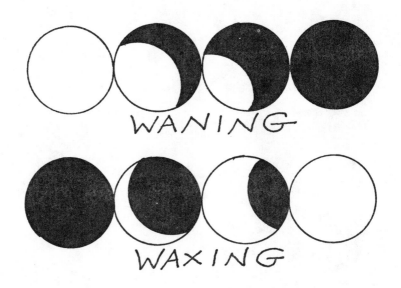

WANING

WAXING

1. Plant vegetables that grow aboveground (such as tomatoes, squash, and lettuce) two nights before the new moon or in the first quarter of the new moon. (She said that this is the first impulse of magnetism.) You can also sow when the moon is waxing from half to full. She also said that, when you sow

38

during the waning moon (from full to smaller size), the seeds won't germinate at all but will wait over to the next period.

2. Plant root crops (such as carrots, beets, radishes, and onions) in the third quarter of the moon when it is waning.

3. Transplant on the waning moon. That way the root will take immediately.

You'll find the dates of particular moon phases in any good almanac. Also, if you'd like more detail, consult the *Moon Sign Book*, edited by Marylee Satren (St. Paul, Minnesota: Llewellyn Publications, 1971).

How Far Apart to Set Plants

No matter where the moon may be, you had better know where your plants are. Spacing is very important in the IPS bed. The object is to set out the plants so that their outer leaves just touch one another when the plants are about three-quarters mature and so that the leaves virtually carpet the bed when fully mature. What happens is that the plants shade their own root zones, allowing the bed to retain moisture (calling for less watering) and ensuring that almost no weeds come through. This area beneath the leaves also creates its own fertile microclimate. At maturity there's virtually a little greenhouse under those leaves. Wind bounces off the foliage, and sunshine glances off. The area doesn't become overhot or overcold or dried out by the wind. This microclimate many gardeners claim is extremely important to good intensive garden beds.

In planting vegetables in the IPS garden, you space the plants a little closer than generally recommended on seed packets or on instructions for seedlings. Corn, for instance, does quite well planted 8 inches apart in IPS gardens (as opposed to the 12 inches apart usually recommended for conventional gardens).

PLANT SPACING IN INCHES

asparagus ... 12	eggplant ... 25	radishes ... 1
beans—bush ... 4	kale ... 16	rhubarb ... 12-36
beans—pole ... 10	lettuce—butterhead ... 4-5	rutabagas ... 6
beets ... 2	lettuce—head ... 10	spinach ... 6
broccoli ... 15	lettuce—leaf ... 5-10	squash—bush ... 18
Brussels sprouts ... 16	melons (supported) 24	Swiss chard ... 4
cabbage ... 12	mustard greens ... 4	tomatoes
carrots ... 1	New Zealand spinach ... 8	(trained in air) ... 18
cauliflower ... 30	okra ... 15	turnips ... 6
corn ... 8	onions ... 2-3	
cucumbers	peas (trained in air) ... 2	
(trained in air) ... 4	peppers ... 14	

How to Start the vegetables

You have a choice as to how you can start your vegetables.

1. For some vegetables, such as carrots, beets, and other roots, you should sow seeds directly in the ground.

2. For broccoli, cabbage, cauliflower, lettuce, onions, tomatoes, and several other vegetables, you can buy seedlings from the nursery and transplant them directly into your garden.

3. For most vegetables, you can plant seeds in containers indoors and then later transplant the resultant seedlings outdoors when the weather warms up.

Now let's take a closer look at each of these methods and see how they work into your own gardening plans.

Sowing Seeds Directly

Where do seeds come from? Well, for most of us they come from the seed racks found in hardware stores, nurseries, dime stores, and elsewhere. Just look over every seed rack you find and pick out the vegetables that look good to you. The varieties found on racks in your area are generally okay for your particular climate.

There are other places to find seeds. Some of us, for instance are incurable seed catalog fans. I have a good friend who starts to send for seed catalogs about December. By January they are piled three or four feet high on his desk. By February 1 they're all over the floor, and by mid-February he's started ordering. Then the packages come in by the dozens. I don't think that he ever plants much; he just loves seed catalogs and can't resist ordering. Seed catalogs are good dream material. (In the appendix you'll find the addresses of several companies that will mail you seed catalogs.)

To get good results with certain plants, you must start with seeds. Such plants as bush beans, beets, carrots, dwarf peas, radishes, rutabagas, spinach, and turnips don't transplant very well, so you'll want to sow their seeds directly into the garden bed. Here's how to do it.

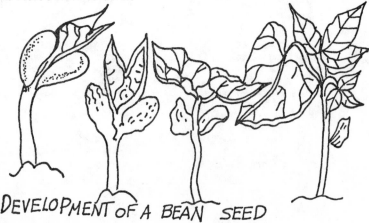

DEVELOPMENT OF A BEAN SEED

1. Soak the soil the day before planting.

2. Scatter the seed evenly across the bed (or a portion of it), and try not to miss the corners. Try to space the seeds roughly according to the spacing table. The bigger seeds—such as those for radishes and spinach—won't be any problem. You can see exactly where they are; and if you get too many in one spot, you can just move them around. With tiny seeds—such as those for carrots—you'll have more of a problem, but you can get the hang of it by practicing with coffee grounds over a piece of paper.

3. Cover the seeds with fine soil. Different vegetable seeds require different depths below the soil surface. Consult the instructions in Chapter 6 for particular vegetables.

4. Later, if too many plants come up, crowding one another, don't worry about it. Just thin them out a bit, pulling up a number of the plants so that the ones that are left are more evenly distributed according to our desired spacing. (You'll get a dividend here, because the small beets and carrots that you pull up can be extra tender and delicious.)

Not all the seeds will come up. Germination is never 100 percent, for a few seeds in any collection will be sterile. Even the germination of fertile seeds is affected by soil moisture, depth of planting, and other conditions that are rarely perfect.

(Unused seeds, by the way, can be saved for the next year. The germination rate will drop only slightly year to year. Simply seal the seed packets airtight with tape and store them in a very cool place.)

IMPROPER

RESULT

Some vegetables—such as broccoli, Brussels sprouts, cabbage, cauliflower, eggplant, peppers, and tomatoes—seem to get off to a better start if they are first grown from seed indoors and then later transplanted into the garden as seedlings. (Lettuce, melons, and onions seem to develop well either way—either from seeds sown directly in the garden or from transplants.) In general, transplanting gives you a head start because you have little plants already developed by the time that it's warm enough outdoors to plant. Also, you avoid having to thin any plants; you space the seedlings directly.

If you decide to buy vegetables as small plants, you can generally find most of the popular varieties at your local nursery or garden center.

When planting seedlings, dig a hole in your IPS bed big enough to avoid bending or squeezing the root mass. Try not to disturb the roots any more than possible when transferring

Buying Seedlings and Transplanting

PROPER

to the ground; and, once the plant is in, make sure that the soil is firm but not packed around the roots.

For transplanting, you can probably get by with a small trowel. But there are other tools that can be useful. One of the best is a pointed stick, just a small dowel with a rounded point. Use it in your left hand to poke in the soil. With your right hand hold the seedling in the hole, and then, with the stick, fill in around the roots and push the soil back.

Starting Seeds Indoors in Containers

Why bother to start your own seeds indoors at all when it's a lot easier to just go down to the nursery, pick out what seedlings you need, and come back and plunk them in your garden? The reasons for developing your own seedlings are both psychological and practical. The psychological reason is purely the joy and feeling of accomplishment of having grown plants from the very moment of germination. The plants are entirely yours. The practical reasons are several: Buying seeds is cheaper than buying seedlings. Only a relatively small selection of vegetable varieties are sold at nurseries; thus if you want to experiment with unusual or new varieties, you must grow your plants from seeds. Finally, seedlings (whether grown yourself or purchased from a nursery) are a great advantage for such warm-weather crops as cucumbers, melons, squash, and tomatoes. They don't do well until the weather warms up and outdoor temperatures stay in the 60s or above; so, by planting them indoors early and transplanting them later, you can get a head start on the weather.

42

Metal Foil Pans. Here's an easy way to start vegetables indoors:

1. Get metal foil pans from a variety or grocery store. To fill them, make up a soil mix of equal parts sand, loam (soil with a lot of organic material), and compost or peat moss. Screen this mixture so that the particles are fairly small. You can also buy prepared planting mixes at any nursery.

2. Plant the seeds an inch or two apart and cover them with soil or vermiculite. Vermiculite—light mineral granules that can be bought packaged at any nursery—is best because it holds moisture well.

3. Place the containers in a warm place (above 60° to 65° F.) where they will be in full sun or under a fluorescent light for about 12 hours a day, if possible. (Just do the best you can.) For fast germination of the seeds of eggplant, peppers, and tomatoes, you'll need a soil temperature of 75° to 85° F. Within a couple of weeks, in any event, most plants will have begun to poke through the soil.

4. When the second pair of leaves opens, move each plant to a separate small pot or to a small paper cup, or space the plants 3 inches apart in another loaf pan.

5. Transplant the seedlings outside according to the dates given earlier in this chapter in the vegetable planting list..

Peat Pots. Peat pots are small individual pots or pellets, square or round, made of compressed peat moss or other materials; you can buy them at any nursery. Some types are already filled with soil; others you must fill with potting soil. Into each pot sow a seed or two; and when the plant is several inches tall, transplant pot and all to the garden bed. The roots

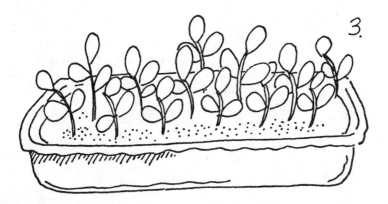

grow through the walls of the pot, and the plants don't suffer any transplant shock. You don't lose any soil from around the roots, and the nutrients are built right into the pot. These peat pots are especially good for cucumber, melons, and squash, because disturbing their roots by transplanting tends to check their growth.

Starter Kits. If using peat pots seems too hard, buy one of those starter kits for tomatoes and other vegetables—the kits that have container, soil, and seeds already all put together. All you have to do is take the lid off the container and water the soil. (Sometimes, though, you'll find the seeds in a separate packet that you sow yourself.)

Flats. You can also start seeds in a flat; a good size is a 14-by-24-inch box about 3 inches deep. Use the soil mix of sand, loam, and compost or peat moss described above, or buy big packages of planting soil. Soak the soil in the flat thoroughly. For small seeds, sow gently over the surface, then press in. For larger seeds, make furrows with a pencil, the furrows to be 2 inches apart and at the depth required for particular vegetables. Then drop in your seeds and cover with soil. Place the flat in a warm light spot—like that described for metal foil pans above. When the first two sets of leaves have developed, transplant the seedlings individually to small pots or to other flats, spacing them 3 inches apart. When transferring seedlings, alway be careful to disturb the roots as little as possible.

Hardening the Transplants. Before actually planting the young seedlings in the soil outdoors, you should get them used to outdoor conditions. Adjust the young plants to outdoor temperatures by putting them outdoors (in their containers) when it's sunny. Bring them indoors whenever frost seems likely, especially overnight. In one way or another, expose them to the lower temperatures for about two weeks before setting them out in your garden bed.

There are, of course, more complicated methods of growing young seedlings for transplanting, but in this book I'm dedicated to giving you the easiest ways possible that work well with the least hassle.

Other Seeding Methods

It's also possible to plant outdoors before the weather really gets warm enough to expose particular plants fully to the elements. For melons, for instance, you can make small frames or boxes, each 1 foot by 1 foot and 3 or 4 inches high, with a clear vinyl plastic cover, and place them on your prepared garden bed. Plant 8 to 10 seeds within each frame. Remove the plastic cover on warm days; replace it on cold nights or days. Remove the cover entirely when the danger of frost has passed.

Another idea is to make "jug houses" for your plants by cutting off the bottoms of gallon bottles and setting the bottomless jugs over your planted seeds. Or you can simply buy commercially made waxed-paper plant protectors (often called hot caps) from a nursery. All of these methods will give your seedlings a faster start. Just make sure that you remove the hot caps, jugs, or plastic sheets on warm days, or they're liable to burn under those coverings that intensify heat.

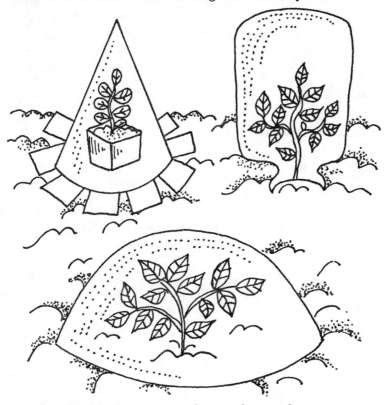

You probably know a gardener who produces so many vegetables out of his small garden that you wonder if he isn't hauling them in from the country. He isn't. He's just mastered those little tricks that makes mother nature work overtime.

These miracle "crop stretchers" are intercropping, succession planting, and catch cropping.

How to Stretch Your Crops

Intercropping

Intercropping simply means planting quick-maturing crops between slower-maturing crops. With intercropping you can plant quick-maturing radishes, green onions, or leaf lettuce between rows of corn or tomatoes. Because you plant corn and tomatoes far apart—8 inches for corn and 18 inches for tomatoes—you will harvest the intercrops before the corn and tomato plants have become big enough to crowd the smaller plants out. That's getting double duty out of your IPS bed.

Succession Planting

Succession planting consists in planting a later crop as soon as you take out an early one. (Make sure that you add compost, manure, bone meal, and wood ash, or their substitutes, before you do replant, however.) For instance, harvest spinach and then plant beans, or take out broccoli and then plant corn. Or plant early, midseason, and late-maturing varieties of the same kind of vegetable. Any combination of early and late varieties stretches the productivity of your garden. Here are some suggestions for succession planting:

Beets—followed by Brussels sprouts

Snap beans—followed by cabbage, cauliflower, kale, lettuce, or spinach.

Peas—followed by beans

Catch Cropping

Catch cropping consists in planting quick-maturing plants in places from which you've just harvested larger, slower-growing vegetables. You can harvest a couple of broccoli plants in late summer, for instance, and then grow radishes or green onions in the very same space.

The basic rule here is simply: Don't leave bare ground unplanted.

CHAPTER SIX

Basic Vegetables That You'll Love to Grow and a Few Others That You'll Probably Want to Try

What vegetables should you grow in your IPS garden?

That depends a lot on you. What you really need to do when selecting vegetables is to consider what vegetables you like and whether or not those particular vegetables are suited to the space that you have available. It's also important, of course, to select varieties that grow well in your geographical area, but generally anything purchased from local seed racks will do reasonably well.

A very important consideration is that some vegetables grow well in small gardens and some don't.

If you're planting a 6-by-6-foot garden, a pumpkin vine or a large squash vine just won't do.

I have a friend who purchased a couple of packages of Big Max pumpkin seeds, took them home, and planted them in a backyard flower bed. By July the pumpkin vine had taken over most of that bed and had spread ten feet down the sidewalk. The family didn't use the backyard much, however (it was 10 by 40 feet), so they left the vines alone. By late August the plant had filled almost the entire backyard and had grown two medium-sized pumpkins about two feet across. (That's medium-sized for a Big Max.) In my friend's case it was okay. But in most Intensive Postage Stamp gardens, Big Max would create a disaster.

In this chapter I include all vegetables that grow well in IPS gardens and a few that are just marginally acceptable. The marginal ones, like cabbage and asparagus, are here because they're old favorites and can be grown if you're willing to put up with a few special conditions.

In an IPS garden you must consider how much ground the vegetables take up and just how long they tie up that space. Most pumpkins and winter squash, for instance, have large vines that run all over the place. Potatoes take up only about a square foot per plant, but they tie up the ground a good four months. Better buy them at the supermarket. The same is true of parsnips (four months), celery (four to six months), and a few others. They are all great vegetables in their own right, but they are just not suitable for the type of high-yield gardening that we're taking up in this book. Thus they are omitted from this chapter.

One popular fad has been to grow so-called midget vegetables. The midget vegetables, whose miniature plants are one-half to one-fifth the size of those for regular vegetables, are space savers all right; and there are now quite a few of them around: cabbage, corn, cucumbers, lettuce, melons, and so on. The only problem is that if you're looking for quantity, you'll have to grow twice or three times as many of these midgets to obtain the same production that you would get from regular-sized plants. Try them if you like, but I'd just as soon plant the other varieties in my own garden.

Harvesting. When considering individual vegetables, you should also begin to think ahead to picking them. Actually I never really make much of a deal out of harvesting my vegetables. When I'm ready to eat something I just go out and pick, although I probably pay for this haphazardness with a flavor loss. After all, there is a right and a wrong time to pick vegetables. Many plants go through a chemical change converting sugar to starch (this is especially true of corn). The trick is to catch them when the sugar (or flavor) content is highest. The general rule is to try to pick vegetables before they're completely mature and then cook them as soon as possible. Vegetables picked this way are far tastier than anything you can buy in the supermarket, because by the time vegetables travel from the commercial grower, to the wholesale market, to the store, and then to you the best part of the flavor has already been lost.

In the list of "popular varieties" under each vegetable in this chapter, I give the days to maturity—that is, the average length of time that it takes vegetables to ripen, from planting to maturity. The figures are averages only and are affected by sunniness, cloudiness, temperatures, and other climatic variables in different regions of the country. Moreover, seed cataloguers aren't always clear on what the figures mean. For most vegetables the maturity days denote the period of time from planting seeds outdoors to harvesting. But for some vegetables, such as tomatoes, peppers, and eggplant, the maturity days denote the period of time from planting seedlings outdoors to harvesting; this period has, of course, been preceded by four to eight weeks of indoor growing.

Home storage. Fresh vegetables can be stored in your home for long periods provided that you have storage areas of proper temperatures and proper dampness or dryness. As a general rule, the cooler you keep vegetables the better. Individual vegetables, however, have their own temperature and humidity requirements.

Beets, carrots, turnips, and rutabagas like lots of moisture and a temperature between 34° and 42° F. You can store these root vegetables in a damp cellar or possibly in a cool garage, preferably in a container like a garbage can with rags on top of the vegetables that you wet down occasionally.

Cabbage stores best with a moderate amount of moisture and a temperature between 48° and 62° F. Individual squash should be spread out so that air can circulate between them.

Freezing Vegetables. There are a few general rules that you should follow when preparing vegetables for freezing.

First you should wash the vegetables in cold water.

Most vegetables must then be immersed in boiling water for two to four minutes in order to halt the enzyme action that causes vegetables to lose flavor and become tough. This parboiling is called blanching.

Immediately after removing the vegetables from the boiling water, plunge them into a pan of ice water, leaving them in the pan until they're cool.

Finally, before placing the vegetables in the freezer, pack them in some kind of container. You can use heavy plastic bags sealed with rubber bands or wire twists; empty milk cartons or other wax-lined containers sealed with tape; or simply plastic freezer containers that can be purchased at most supermarkets and variety stores.

(In the remainder of this chapter you'll find more specific instructions for individual vegetables.)

Now, with these matters out of the way, let's take a look at the individual vegetables and see how they fit into our Intensive Postage Stamp garden.

Asparagus

Cool season crop. Rated marginal for IPS gardens.

Unlike most other vegetables, which are annuals, asparagus is a perennial plant; and, once it's planted and gets going, it just keeps right on pouring out a continuous food supply every season for the next fifteen years or so.

Planting. Actually, asparagus is not the best plant for an IPS garden because it tends to take over and eat up space. But if you're an asparagus lover as I am, you'll find a way to sneak it in somewhere. You definitely, however, don't want your asparagus in a small IPS bed with other vegetables. You can successfully grow it alone in a 4-by-4-foot IPS bed surrounded by a frame. Grown this way, it stays fairly well within boundaries. Asparagus also does extremely well in a flower bed because its ornamental fronds blend in nicely.

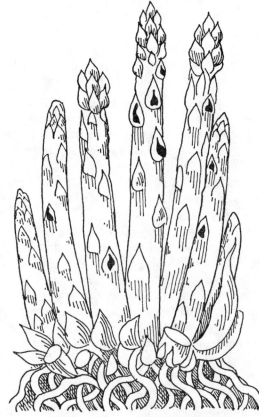

You can start asparagus from seed, but if you do, you'll throw away a whole year right there. Grown from seeds, it will not produce its first crop until the third year. Therefore, you had best buy one-year-old roots from your local nursery and transplant them directly into the garden. Even using roots, you will not get a crop until the second year.

In some ways, asparagus and the IPS bed were made for each other. Asparagus demands rich, loose soil that's nice and deep; and that's exactly what we have. In early spring just plant the roots about 12 inches apart. That's pretty close for asparagus, but it seems to work out all right. For each plant make a hole about 5 inches in diameter, 8 inches deep. At the bottom of the hole, spread out the roots, crown side up, and cover with 2 inches of soil. As the plant grows, simply keep filling the hole with additional soil; but *do not cover the crown tip.* Two to three months after planting, the hole should have been filled to ground level.

Unfortunately, asparagus doesn't grow nearly so fast as other vegetables; and, although you'll get some spears the first year, don't cut them, but let them go to foliage. When they turn brown in the fall, cut them to the ground. The second year, though, you can harvest spears for about four weeks. The year after, you can cut spears for eight to ten weeks.

Feed asparagus with fish emulsion a couple of times a year. (Apply according to the instructions on the bottle.)

Crop Stretching. Asparagus is extremely prolific without much help.

Popular Varieties. Be sure to choose rust-resistant varieties of asparagus. Here are a few that are successful:

Mary Washington	Thick, heavy, dark-green shoots, good flavor, old-time favorite
Waltham Washington	Spears uniform in size, a heavy producer
California 500	Pleasant-flavored, not stringy, easy to raise

Typical Problems. You'll have few problems with asparagus—except for insect pests, which we take up in Chapter 8.

Harvesting. When the asparagus spears are 8 to 10 inches long and when the buds at the tips are still compressed, you can harvest by cutting the spears at ground level or a few inches below. You can also snap the spears off by bending them over sharply until they break.

To freeze asparagus, use only the tender portions (the tops and smaller shoots) and prepare them immediately. Blanch them in boiling water 2 to 4 minutes, cool rapidly, place in containers, and freeze.

Beans   *Warm season crop. Rated good to excellent for IPS gardens.*

Bean plants are literally small food factories that really give you your money's worth in the IPS garden. In addition, they do double duty, because they're one of the legumes (peas being the other major variety), which help to improve the fertility of the soil. What happens is that bacteria living in the nodules on the roots of legumes take soil nitrogen in unusable forms and combine it with sugars from the legumes to produce ammonia, a nitrogen compound that plants can use. Legumes thus actually conserve and restore the soil.

Primarily there are two types of beans grown by home gardeners, snap and lima. (Snaps are also called string beans, green beans, or wax beans. Limas are sometimes called butter beans.) Both snaps and limas come in bush varieties, which grow 15 to 20 inches tall, and in pole or climbing varieties, which grow as vines up poles 5 to 8 feet high. Some people recommend bush beans for small gardens, because they mature in less than 60 days and will grow three or four plants in every square foot of space.

Planting. Beans are heat lovers, so plant the seeds after the ground has warmed up in the spring. Plant seeds of bush types 1 inch deep and about 4 inches apart, and pole beens 1 inch deep and about 10 inches apart. Make plantings every two weeks (until about 60 days before the first fall frost) in order to harvest beans all summer long. Beans need lots of water and shouldn't be allowed to dry out while they're still growing.

In an IPS garden the nutrients that you've already put in the soil will carry your beans through the season, but they'll do better if you give them some fish emulsion just as the pods begin to form. (Apply according to the instructions on the bottle.)

Crop Stretching. Although horizontal space in the IPS garden is tight, you have almost unlimited vertical space. Therefore, the more you can get your plants up in the air the more food your garden will crank out. Here are some methods that work well for beans:

1. Set up four 6-foot posts (preferably 2 by 2s) at the corners of a one square foot of space. Plant two seeds per pole; the vines twine up the pole. It's possible to place two or three of these plantings around the garden.

2. Set up a 6-foot post (again a 2 by 2) and at the top affix two 1-foot crossarms at right angles to each other. From the ends of these crossarms run strings or wires to the bottom of the post. Plant 4 to 6 seeds around the post. The vines twine up the strings or wires.

3. Between two 6-foot posts (preferably 4 by 4s), spaced about 6 feet apart, run a sheet of chicken wire, creating a kind of trellis or fence. Along the fence, plant seeds about 8 inches apart, and train the vines up the chicken wire.

Varieties.
Bush green

Tendercrop	53 days	Dark green, slender pods
Topcrop	49 days	Medium green, hardy
Bush Blue Lake	58 days	Dark-green pods, heavy yielder
Spartan Arrow	52 days	Pods in clusters
Greensleeves	56 days	Dark-green pods, white-seeded
Bush wax		
Burpee's Brittle Wax	52 days	Lemon-yellow pods, hardy, prolific

Bush purple

Royalty Purple Pod	51 days	Purple pods that cook green, good in colder soils

Pole snap

Kentucky Wonder	65 days	Large green pods, heavy producer
Blue Lakes	59 days	Bright dark green, fleshy, good for freezing or canning
Ramone	70 days	Wide-podded, green beans, heavy producer

Bush lima

Fordhook 242	75 days	Big-seeded
Henderson Bush	65 days	Flat pods, small beans, withstands hot weather
Baby Fordhook Bush Lima	70 days	Thick-seeded

Pole lima

King of the Garden	88 days	Pods about 5 inches long, old favorite
Prizetaker	90 days	Large beans, good quality

Bush shell beans

Red Kidney	95 days	Large kidney-shaped beans, stalks 20-22 inches tall

A novelty to try

Yard Long (Asparagus Bean)	70 days	Actually a variety of cowpea, rather than a bean; pods grow up to 4 feet long; seeds can be ordered from Henry Field or Burgess (see catalog list in appendix)

Typical Problems. My vines don't produce well. Sometimes the bean ends shrivel up.

They are probably not getting enough water. Beans need considerable water and shouldn't ever dry out while growing. When there isn't enough moisture in the soil, the bean ends will sometimes shrivel up. Also, you may not be picking the young beans as they mature; old pods left on the vine will cut the production of new ones.

54

My beans didn't come up at all.

You probably planted before the soil warmed up. Bean seeds won't germinate in cold soil, nor will they come up well if the soil has crusted over. A sprouting bean seed must push the small stem and leaves through the soil; if the ground is too hard at the surface, it can't do this. (This generally isn't a problem in an IPS garden because we made it nice and loose and grainy before planting.)

Beans can also get in trouble if they are not well fertilized. But we've already handled this adequately, so if you give them a little supplement of fish emulsion about halfway through, that should do the trick.

Harvesting. Pick beans when they're fairly small. The flavor of small beans is better, and keeping the plants picked helps extend the bearing season.

Freeze only the small tender beans. Remove their ends, cut them in small lengths, blanch in boiling water for 1½ minutes, cool, place in containers, and freeze.

Cool season crop. Rated excellent for IPS gardens.   **Beets**

Beets are double-barreled vegetables; that is, you can eat both the roots and the leaves, and both are delicious. Beets are probably an almost perfect vegetable for the IPS garden, because they don't take up much room and they grow like mad. (I've produced as many as 400 beets in a 4-by-4-foot area.)

Planting. Beets generally like cool weather, but they're also fairly tolerant of a wide temperature range. Once started, beets need to grow rapidly without stopping, which means that you've got to keep them watered.

In an IPS bed you scatter seed 1 inch apart and ½ inch deep, but be careful with beet seeds because, unlike most other vegetables, they come in clumps of three or more seeds (called seedballs) that produce three or more plants. This means that it's awfully easy to sow too many. Simply thin out the little plants as you go along, and cook up the young beet greens. You'll probably also want to divide your beet area into quarters, planting each quarter every five to ten days to ensure a continuous harvest.

Crop Stretching. Plant beets in any spot where you've taken out another vegetable—corn, for instance.

Popular Varieties. You have a choice of globe-shaped, semiglobe-shaped, and yellow beets, as well as beets used mostly for greens.

Red globe

Detroit Dark Red	59 days	Dark red, roots of uniform globe shape, excellent for greens
Ruby Queen	60 days	Fast growth

Semiglobe

Early Wonder	55 days	Dark red, smooth-skinned

Beets for greens

Lutz Green Leaf	80 days	Glossy green tops, sweet

Novelties to Try

Burpee Golden	55 days	Golden, good in salads
Burpee White	60 days	White, tender, excellent for greens

Typical Problems. My beets tasted woody.
The plants are not getting enough moisture. As with most other vegetables, you have to keep beets growing full blast until they mature. Lack of water will slow them down and make them woody.

My beets didn't get very big.
You sowed too many seeds and forgot to thin. Thin the small plants, leaving only one plant every inch or so.

Harvesting. Pick beets when small (just pick one to see how big they have grown). Big beets get tough and taste blah.

For freezing, pick small beets, peel them, blanch in boiling water 4½ to 5 minutes, cool, place in containers, and freeze. Large beets can also be frozen, but they usually lack flavor.

Broccoli   *Cool season crop. Rated good for IPS gardens.*
You might call broccoli the IPS gardener's best friend in the cabbage family. It's big. After all, it can grow 3 or 4 feet high and branch prolifically. Also, it's easy to grow, and once it gets started it just keeps

right on producing for a month or two. All you have to do is cut off the terminal head and the side shoots start to develop in small clusters right away. It's also possible to grow some of the other members of the cabbage family in our IPS garden, but they tend to be overlarge, and we have to be very selective in handling them.

Planting. Being a cool weather plant, broccoli can be a problem because it's pretty sensitive to heat. It'll grow like mad, then all of a sudden—during a heat wave—begin to flower. After that, it's all over as a vegetable.

Buy broccoli from your nursery as small plants. This is the standard planting method, because starting from seeds will take you several weeks longer to get a mature vegetable. Four to six plants are about all that an IPS garden can handle, because they must be spaced 15 inches apart. You can plant them in the spring a couple of weeks before the last frost, then again in midsummer. Midsummer is probably the best time because the weather will have cooled by the time the plants reach maturity.

If you prefer starting from seeds, plant them indoors in peat pots ¼ inch deep about five to six weeks before you intend to set the plants outside. (The other indoor planting methods described in Chapter 5 can also be used.)

Broccoli, like other members of the cabbage family, is a heavy feeder, so give it some fish emulsion at least once before the heads begin to form. (Apply according to the instructions on the bottle.)

Crop Stretching. Replace harvested broccoli with carrots, beets, or radishes.

Popular Varieties.

Green Comet	55 days	Extra-large heads, early
Spartan Early	55 days	Good-sized solid-center heads, early
Waltham 29	74 days	Long harvest period, late, for fall use

Typical Problem. My broccoli flowers before the heads are ready to harvest.

You're getting too much heat. If you're having trouble with your spring crop, try planting in midsummer for a fall crop. In mild winter areas, where the temperatures generally don't drop below freezing, you can plant broccoli from early fall through late winter.

Harvesting. Broccoli is ready to cut when the tops are hard and green, just before the buds begin to open. You simply cut the stem a few leaves below the main head. The bud-shoots that subsequently form in the leaf joints below the cut will never get more than an inch or two across, but they can be harvested and eaten. If your plants are kept picked, your growing season will continue until warm weather arrives —or, in the fall, until frost.

For freezing broccoli, use the tender portions only. Trim off the woody parts, cut the clusters into small pieces, blanch them in boiling water for 2 to 3 minutes, cool rapidly, place in containers, and freeze.

Brussels Sprouts

Cool season crop. Rated fair for some IPS gardens.

One Brussels sprouts plant will keep producing sprouts until you wonder if it's ever going to stop (one plant will produce seventy-five to a hundred sprouts). Brussels sprouts are a member of the cabbage family and are an erect plant that produces ever-growing clusters of sprouts or buds in the axils of the leaves. They're easy to grow—if you live in the right climate.

Planting. Brussels sprouts are a cool weather plant. They do extremely well for you if you live in an area of summer fog, or in an area where the climate is nice and moist and summer daytime temperatures generally average 65° F. or less. They don't do well where the climate is hot and dry.

Because Brussels sprouts take quite a lot of space, you probably won't want more than one or two in any single IPS garden. Set the plants out in early summer so that they mature in the colder fall weather. If you have mild winters, with above-freezing temperatures, you can also plant them in the fall for winter harvest.

Most gardeners buy young plants from their local nursery. Set the plants 16 inches apart. As the plants mature, remove all excess leaves except those at the top of the plant.

You can grow Brussels sprouts from seed if you like, but you should start them indoors, planting your seeds ½ inch deep in peat pots five or six weeks before you intend to set them outdoors.

Crop Stretching. Interchange Brussels sprouts with quick- or early-maturing crops, such as radishes and leaf lettuce.

Popular Varieties.

Jade Cross Hybrid	80 days	Blue-green sprouts, 22-inch plants
Long Island Improved	90 days	Dark-green heads

Typical Problems. Practically none, other than the weather restrictions already noted.

Harvesting. Pick the lowest sprouts each time you pick, and break off any leaves left below the "sprout." Don't remove the top leaves.

For freezing, first wash the Brussels sprouts and then soak them ½ hour in salted water (1 teaspoon salt per quart of water). Place them in clear water and bring just to a boil. Then drain, chill rapidly, and freeze.

Cool season crop. Rated marginal for IPS gardens.

Cabbage

Cabbage often turns out to be a big show-off. It comes in green, red, and purple varieties and is a great conversation piece grown singly in a prominent spot. The only complaint that I have about cabbage is that it takes an awful lot of space for what you get out of it. If you insist on cabbage, you might plant three or four in an IPS garden, or put one by itself in a flower bed where it can be ornamental.

Planting. Cabbage is a cool weather plant, so you want to time your plantings so that the plants reach maturity before or after the hot summer months. Put the plants out in the early spring or in late summer.

Most gardeners buy small seedlings from a nursery rather than start from seeds. The seedlings should be set 12 inches apart in your IPS bed.

If you want to start cabbage from seed, sow the seeds ½ inch deep in flats or peat pots about six to eight weeks before you intend to set the plants outdoors.

New cabbage plants should never be set where other cabbages or any cabbage relatives have been grown in the past two or three years. This precaution is necessary in order to reduce the risk of being plagued by common cabbage diseases.

Crop Stretching. You can follow beans with a planting of cabbage. Also you can make successive plantings of cabbage to stretch the season.

Popular Varieties.

Early

Early Jersey Wakefield	63 days	Conical heads, 2-3 pounds
Golden Acre	63 days	Medium, 4-5 pounds
Copenhagen Market	72 days	Medium, 4-4½ pounds

Late

Danish Ball-head	105 days	Weighs more for size than any other cabbage

Red

Red Acre	76 days	Deep red, medium-sized
Red Head	85 days	Richly colored, midseason

Savoy

Chieftain Savoy	90 days	Firm head

Midget

Dwarf Morden	53 days	4-inch heads, 1 pound

Typical Problem. My cabbage heads split badly.
Cabbage needs a good steady supply of water. Any time that the watering becomes irregular, growth becomes irregular—slowing down, resuming, slowing down again. This causes the cabbage to crack. Therefore, you should make sure that you keep your cabbages supplied with water. If you haven't, however, you can try a reverse trick. You can *delay* growth and halt cracking by holding off on the water when cracking begins, or you can twist the plant to break off some of the roots and thereby slow the growth process.

Harvesting. Pick cabbage heads as soon as the heads feel solid. If you let them mature on the plant, the core gradually lengthens until it bursts through the top and uncurls into a long stalk.
Cabbage does not freeze well.

Cool season crop. Rated excellent for IPS gardens. **Carrots**

When the ancient Greeks and Romans used carrots for medicine, but wouldn't eat them for food, they really goofed, because carrots supply more food in our gardens over a longer period of time than practically anything else. They're also super-packed with vitamins—A, B_1, small amounts of B_2, and C—as well as sugar and iron.

Carrots, like beets, need to grow fast, so make sure that they have plenty of water and never dry out.

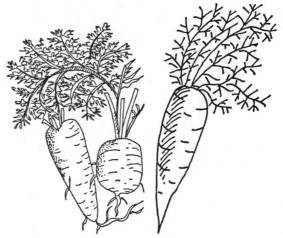

Planting. Carrots are more tolerant of garden mistakes than almost any other plant that I can think of. They are generally considered a cool season crop—best for spring and fall—but they do pretty well all summer, maturing sixty-five to seventy-five days after initial planting.

For a season-long crop, divide your planting area into quarters, and then scatter seed in each quarter 10 days apart. Cover the seeds with ½ inch of soil. When the tops show, thin the plants to 1 inch apart; a couple of weeks later, thin to 2 inches apart. The tender young carrots are delicious, cooked or raw.

Crop Stretching. As you pull out a few heads of cabbage or broccoli, plant a few carrots in the same space.

Popular Varieties. With carrots you can go wild and plant almost any shape you desire—from very short and almost round to long and slender.

Very short

Ox-Heart	65 days	Roots 5½ to 6 inches long, 3½ to 4 inches across the top; deep-red flesh

Short medium

Red Cored Chantenay	70 days	6 inches long, 2½ inches thick; tender and sweet; orange scarlet
Royal Chantenay	70 days	Broad-shouldered, rich orange
Spartan Bonus	75 days	6-7 inches long, deep orange

Long slender

Gold Pak	76 days	8-9 inches long, 1½ inches across; rich orange
Imperator	75 days	8-9 inches long, 1½ inches across

A novelty to try

Little Finger	65 days	Baby carrot, 3½ inches long

Typical Problem. My carrots just don't germinate well. I'll get a few in a clump in one area, and none in another.

Carrot germination can be a problem. Some of this is due to the seeds drying out. To reduce evaporation, some gardeners recommend placing a black plastic sheet over the carrot bed immediately after sowing, then removing it as the seedlings start to break through. You must watch carefully, however, in order to make sure to remove the plastic before it stunts the seedlings.

Harvesting. Pick carrots when relatively small. Big carrots produce woody cores.

For real flavor, plant a few more than you need; then thin them when they're big enough to eat.

For freezing, small carrots are best, but you can cut the big ones into small pieces. Blanch the carrots in boiling water about 3 minutes, cool quickly, pack in containers, and freeze.

Cauliflower

Cool season crop. Rated marginal for IPS gardens.

Cauliflower can be a bit finicky about the weather. In the area where I live it can be cool for awhile during the spring, then suddenly hot; and under these conditions cauliflower just doesn't do very well. But if you live in an area of cool or gradually warming springs or cool summers, your cauliflower should do fine.

Planting. If you live where the spring is fairly cool, but frost-free, you can set out the plants in early spring. If summers are very warm where you live, then you may want to grow your cauliflower in the fall; just set out the plants in late July or early August.

You can grow cauliflower indoors from seed in flats if you like, but it generally takes about 50 days before the plants are ready to set out—an awfully long time. For this reason you should probably buy seedlings from a nursery. Plant them 2½ feet apart.

When the cauliflower begins to head, you must "blanch" the buds—that is, keep them from turning green—by shielding the head from the sun. You do this by pulling a few outer leaves over the head

completely, gathering the tops of these leaves together, and tying them together loosely with a string or rubber band. For purple-headed cauliflower this blanching is unnecessary.

Crop Stretching. If you plant cauliflower in an IPS bed, be sure to grow something else between the plants—radishes or lettuce, for instance. When the radishes or lettuce come out, plant bush beans. This way you'll use all the space efficiently; your cauliflower will be out of the way before your beans are ready to harvest.

Popular Varieties.

Early Snowball	60 days	Firm, deep, globular heads
Snow King Hybrid	50 days	Flattish heads, creamy white, fairly heat tolerant
Purple Head	85 days	Large heads, deep purple on top (don't blanch head)

Typical Problem. My cauliflower heads are always small.
You probably have a watering problem. It's important that you don't check the growth of cauliflower at any time. This can happen if you water irregularly, or don't water for long periods of time. You must water consistently and fairly deeply, and in very hot weather a gentle overhead misting is beneficial too.

Harvesting. Pick cauliflower as soon as the heads fill out; otherwise they will lose quality.
To freeze cauliflower, break the buds into small pieces, blanch them in boiling water for 3 minutes, cool, place in containers, and freeze.

Corn

Warm season crop. Rated fair for IPS gardens.

What we call corn today is a far cry from the maize that the Pilgrims found the Indians growing when they first arrived in America. The reason: corn loves to crossbreed; and, unlike some other plants, every time you cross one kind of corn with another you get something different—in between. As a result, over the last 150 years corn hybridizers have developed countless varieties, and today you have a huge choice: you can plant tall varieties, short varieties, whites, yellows, blacks, popcorn, early varieties, late varieties, and seemingly everything else.

Planting. Corn is a heat lover, so plant the seeds or seedlings after the ground has warmed up. It also needs plenty of water throughout the growing season, and it's a heavy feeder. Generally, IPS soil has enough nutrients to carry corn through a full season; but just to make sure, I sometimes make one feeding of fish emulsion when the plants are about 15 inches tall. (Apply according to the instructions on the bottle.)

Corn isn't terribly good in an IPS garden because it takes up a lot of space from two and a half to three months or more. If you like corn as much as I do, however, you can make up a special 4-by-4-foot bed for corn and plant seedlings in it 8 inches apart. (If you use seeds, plant them 1 inch deep, 8 inches apart.) If possible, you might distribute about three of these 4-by-4 squares somewhere around the yard, planting each square a couple of weeks apart for a continuous crop. Each square will yield about seventy-two ears.

The 4-by-4-foot beds are good because corn is a wind pollinator, and small blocks like these are better than a long row. The reason: corn is a member of the grass family; the tassels contain the male parts, and the silks that come out of the ears are part of the female flowers. Wind-borne pollen from the tassels of one plant falls on the silks of another plant, and each silk that receives pollen produces a mature kernel. Because the pollen can't float very far, the plants must be fairly close together to pollinate one another.

Crop Stretching. Fast-maturing crops such as radishes and lettuce can be planted between your corn, and they'll be harvested before the corn gets tall.

Corn and pole beans can be planted at the same time, close together; and the bean vines will then twine up the cornstalks.

Popular Varieties. You'll generally want to plant either a white variety or a yellow one or both, but not both in the same bed, because if pollen from white corn lands on the silks of yellow (or vice versa), you'll get a crazy mixed-up ear wtih a muddle of whites and yellows.

If you've got a sweet tooth, try the Extra Sweet and Early Sweet varieties. A great variety for IPS gardens is Butterfingers; it matures fairly rapidly and grows about five feet tall.

If you're an experimenter, try one of the two-tone varieties (yellow and white together), such as Butter and Sugar. If you just want to play around with something wild instead of producing food, try ornamental Indian squaw corn. Or try strawberry corn; its kernels have the shape and size much like real strawberries; you can use it for decoration or pop it.

Here are a few varieties:

Yellow

Early Sunglow	63 days	4-5 feet high, stays tender a long time
Royal Crest	64 days	6 feet high
Butterfinger	66 days	Early, golden yellow kernels, supersweet, 5 feet high, good for narrow spacing, good vigor in cold weather
Earliking	66 days	5½ feet high, extrasweet, vigorous
Early Xtra Sweet	71 days	Early, 4-6 feet high, stays sweet over a long period
Jubilee	80 days	Early, 7-7½ feet high, deep narrow yellow kernels, high-yielding
Golden Cross Bantam	85 days	Midseason, 6-7 feet high, golden kernals, high-yielding
Iochief	89 days	Late, 6½ feet high, golden kernels, high-yielding
Seneca Chief	82 days	5-6 feet high, top quality sweet corn
Sundance	69 days	Early, 5-6 feet high, grows vigorously in cool weather

White

Silver Queen	92 days	Late, 7-8 feet high, large ears
Country Gentleman	92 days	Midseason, 7 feet high, sweet white slender kernels
Silver Sweet	65 days	Early, 6 feet high, tender, bright purple husks

Bicolor

Sugar and Gold	67 days	Early, 4-6 feet high, yellow and white kernels
Butter and Sugar	78 days	Late, 6 feet high
Honey and Cream	78 days	5-6 feet high, high yielder

Midgets

Golden Midget	65 days	2-3 feet high, ears 4½ inches long, good for freezing
White Midget	74 days	2½-3 feet tall, sweet, tender

Novelties to Try

Strawberry Ornamental Popcorn	105 days	Highly decorative for table displays and popcorn; tiny mahogany-red ears 2 inches long
Rainbow	110 days	Decorative corn; red, yellow, orange, and blue in many combinations

There are, of course, many more varieties. If in doubt, ask your nurseryman which ones are best for your area.

Typical Problems. I just didn't get very many ears from my few plants.

Corn is a wind pollinator, so it's best to plant a lot together rather than just a few plants.

The lower leaves of my corn turned yellow.

This doesn't happen often if you've made up your IPS soil right, because this condition indicates a nitrogen deficiency. You might give the plants a feeding of fish emulsion (according to the directions on the bottle).

When I husk the ears to cook them, quite often some of the kernels have been eaten by a fairly large worm.

This is the corn earworm. We'll take this up in Chapter 8 when we talk about pests in the garden.

Harvesting. Corn is one of the hardest vegetables to pick properly. You want to catch it in the milky stage. For best results, just take your thumbnail and squeeze a kernel; if it's just right it'll squirt a milky juice. Corn reaches a peak of sweetness, then holds it only two to five days. After that, the sugar starts to turn to starch. Moreover, the minute you pick corn, the sugar in the ear starts to turn to starch. Thus, if you're really looking for top flavor, you've got to pop it in boiling water almost immediately.

For freezing, pick slightly immature yellow corn. If you're freezing corn on the cob, blanch in boiling water 6 to 8 minutes, cool, put in freezer bags, and freeze. If you're going to cut the kernels off the cob, blanch the cob first for 1½ minutes, then cut the kernels off the cob, cool them, package, and freeze.

Cucumbers

Warm season crop. Rated good to excellent for IPS gardens.

Here's a vegetable that undoubtedly is a contender for best actor on the vegetable circuit. Cucumbers have a thousand faces, and if you grow enough different kinds, you'll eventually come up with every shape imaginable. Some are warty, some are smooth, some are prickly, others aren't; they're crooked, straight, balloon-shaped, cigar-shaped, blackjack-shaped, peanut-shaped, and more. Moreover, they're big or small or anything in between. In short, cucumbers really perform in your garden. I love them. After all, who wouldn't love a vegetable that is such a big ham.

Cucumber vines are one of those crazy mixed-up plants that drive some of us to fits of frustration. They're what botanists call monoecious; that is, all male flower parts are in one flower, and all female parts in another (though every plant has both male and female flowers). The first ten to twenty flowers that are produced on any plant are males. Even after that, there are ten to twenty male flowers for every female. The cucumbers themselves come only from the female flowers; thus we have these plants producing all those non-productive flowers before they really get down to the business of making vegetables.

Planting. Cucumbers are heat lovers, so wait until the ground has warmed up before planting. Seeds should be planted 1 inch deep and about 4 inches apart if the vines are going to be trained in the air. To get a head start, you can sow the seeds ½ inch deep in peat pots or flats two to four weeks before outdoor planting and then transfer the seedlings into your IPS bed.

Crop Stretching. Cucumbers ordinarily take a lot of space. In fact, they'll run all over the ground if you let them. That's something that you just can't afford in a good postage stamp garden. So you've got to take to the air if you want to grow cucumbers effectively in a small area. There are a lot of ways to go:

1. Run a fence of chicken wire between two 6-foot posts, and let the vines grow up the wires. Generally the north side of the garden is best for this so that the vines won't shade other plants. Allow the main stem of each plant to grow as high as possible; pinch back some of the lateral shoots, but let some shoots grow into branches. Train the branches on the fence, using plastic tape. You can grow the plants about 4 inches apart along the fence.

If you pick the cucumbers when they're fairly small, you won't have to support them with cloth slings or strings. If they get too big, however, they'll drop off or drag down the vine if they aren't supported somehow.

2. Sink a 6-foot post (preferably a 4 by 4) in your garden, and on it space small 18-inch crossbars up and down the sides. Plant four seeds or seedlings around the post. As the vines grow, tie them to the crossbars.

3. You can also use several types of trellises: rectangular trellises 2 or 3 feet high and 2 or 3 feet wide; X-shaped trellises about 3 by 3 feet; and so on. Buy a ready-made trellis from a local nursery, or make one of your own.

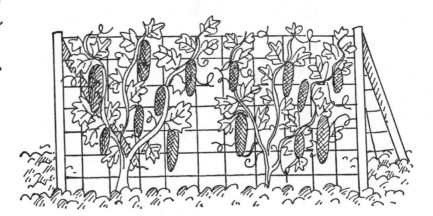

Popular Varieties. With cucumbers you have a choice of those for eating raw or cooked and those for pickling, as well as midget varieties and some in rather unusual shapes, colors, and sizes.

Salads

Early Surecrop	60 days	8 inches long or more
Burpee Hybrid	60 days	Vigorous vines, fruit 8 inches long or more
Marketer	65 days	Extra fancy white, spined
Triumph	57 days	Early bearing, excellent slicer
Ashley	65 days	White spined, fruits well-rounded at ends
Gemini	65 days	Vigorous, heavy yield

Picklers

Spartan Dawn	51 days	Compact vines, abundance of small pickles
Pioneer	51 days	Uniform shape, very tolerant to disease
Wisconsin SMR 18	54 days	Warted pickles that brine well
Crusader	51 days	Medium-green fruit, blunt-ended

Midgets

Tiny Dill Cuke	55 days	Compact vines, finger-length fruit
Patio Pik	57 days	Fruit 4-6½ inches long

Novelties to try

China	75 days	Oriental type, 12 to 15 inches long
Lemon	65 days	Size and color of a lemon, delicious
White Wonder	57 days	All white, bearing early
Armenian Yard Long	65 days	Long, a good slicer

Typical Problems. My cucumbers taste terribly bitter.

Some gardeners say that this is due to uneven watering; others believe it is due to temperature fluctuations of more than 20 degrees daily. If you're having considerable trouble getting a good-tasting cucumber, there is a bitter-free cucumber on the market developed by Cornell University; it's called Marketmore 70. You might try planting it.

The plants just stopped producing new fruit all of a sudden.

You probably left some of the cucumbers to mature on the vines. This can stop a cucumber plant from setting new fruit. Pick cucumbers as soon as they reach usable size.

Harvesting. Pick cucumbers when they're young and green, before the seeds get large and tough.

For pickling recipes, consult *In a Pickle or in a Jam* by Vicki Wilder (Des Moines, Iowa: Better Homes & Gardens Press, 1971).

Eggplant

Warm season crop. Rated fair for IPS gardens.

Here's a garden show-off if I ever saw one—widely grown in the warm regions of the Mediterranean and in India. Eggplants grow on tree-like bushes about two to three feet tall, and most varieties produce beautiful shiny, plumpish, purple-black fruit. Actually, eggplant fruit comes in other shapes and sizes and in colors ranging from purple to yellow to white. The plants are often grown as ornamentals in a garden.

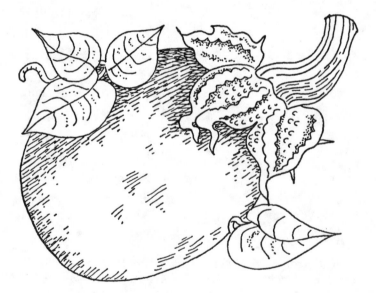

Planting. Eggplant is actually not a good plant for IPS gardens because it takes up so much space, but some gardeners insist on growing one or two. You can plant a few in your flower beds, or you can put a few in one of the 4-by-4-foot framed beds described in Chapter 2.

Because of the long time required to develop eggplants from seeds, most gardeners buy seedlings from nurseries. In your IPS bed set the young plants 25 inches apart, well after the soil has warmed up in the spring.

If you must grow from seeds, you've got to have a lot of patience, for the seeds sometimes take three weeks or more to germinate and then another eight to ten weeks before they're ready to be set out. If this is what you want to do, though, simply sow the seeds ⅓ to ½ inch deep in peat pots and transplant the complete unit, seedling, soil, and pot.

Eggplant is a heat lover and needs to grow steadily and unchecked throughout the summer. This means regular watering. Eggplants are also heavy feeders, and it helps if you give them some fish emulsion about every six weeks. (Apply according to the directions on the bottle.)

Crop Stretching. Grow radishes, lettuce, and similar fast-maturing vegetables in the space around eggplants. They are harvested long before the eggplants mature.

Popular Varieties.

Black

Burpee Hybrid Eggplant	70 days	Tall, semispreading bush
Early Beauty Hybrid	62 days	Early; short, oval fruits
Black Beauty	83 days	Fruit about the size of a cup

A novelty to try

Golden Yellow Eggplant	75 days	Small lemon-sized fruit, gold-colored (can be ordered from Nichols Garden Nursery)

Typical Problem. I planted a few plants in the spring, and they just sat there and did nothing.

You probably planted before it was warm enough. You can protect your small plants by putting a cut-off jug over them or by covering them with "hot caps" bought from a local nursery.

Harvesting. Pick your eggplants before they start to lose their glossy shine; after that, they'll be tough. Be sure to keep picking the fruits as they become ready, so that the plants will continue to bear.

Kale   *Cool season crop. Rated good for IPS gardens.*

Other members of the cabbage family may be a little hard to grow, but not kale, if you grow it in the right season. Kale is a great flower bed crop too because the leaves are so beautiful. They're curled and fringed and range from dark green to bluish purple.

Planting. Kale is a cool weather plant like other cabbage crops and does best under cool conditions. If your summers are cool, with average daytime temperatures of 75° or less, you have no problem. Otherwise, sow your seed in midsummer so that the plants grow in the cool days of fall. Or if your frost-free days begin early in the spring, sow seed for a late spring or early summer crop.

Sow the seeds ½ inch deep, about 16 inches apart. To keep kale coming along well, you should generally give it a feeding of fish emulsion about midseason. (Apply according to the instructions on the label.)

Crop Stretching. You can stretch your harvest by planting kale in place of any crop that matures by midsummer—early corn, for instance.

Popular Varieties.

Dwarf Blue Curled Vates	60 days	Low, compact, withstands below-freezing temperatures
Dwarf Siberian	65 days	Hardy, spreading, 12 to 16 inches tall
Blue Leaf	110 days	Hardy

Typical Problem. My kale isn't doing very well by mid-spring.
Kale is a cool weather crop, remember. It generally does best as a fall crop and doesn't like heat very well.

Harvesting. You can cut the outer leaves as they mature, or cut the entire plant. Generally, the inside leaves are more flavorsome and tender than the outer ones.

Cool season crop. Rated excellent for IPS gardens. **Lettuce**

What a vegetable! You can grow lettuce almost without effort, tuck it in anywhere, take your choice of color or type, and spend hours at the seed racks looking at varieties that you've never seen before.

Lettuce, of course, is well known as the dieter's friend. It is chock-full of vitamins A and B and yet contains almost no calories. What more could you ask?

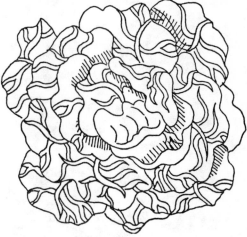

Planting. You can start lettuce from either seeds or plants (the plants can be purchased from a nursery or grown yourself). If you want head lettuce as soon as possible in the spring, start seeds indoors in a pot (¼ to ½ inch deep) about two weeks before the last frost. When all danger of frost has passed, start setting the plants out in the garden. At the same time, you can plant more seeds in the garden bed itself (¼ to ½ inch deep) for a later crop.

Set head lettuce about 10 inches apart, butterhead 4 or 5 inches apart. The spacing for leaf lettuce and romaine can vary. If you intend to pick the outer leaves over a period of time (letting the core of the plant continue to grow), then plant the lettuce 10 inches apart. If you intend to pick the entire plant at once, 4 inches is okay. You'll get more that way.

When summers are hot, plant lettuce in partial shade or give it protection with a lath or gauze on a frame. Lettuce, remember, is a cool season crop. In hot areas, the longer days and warmer nights of summer encourage flowering (bolting to seed). You can correct this problem somewhat by planting varieties that are slow to bolt.

Crop Stretching. You can plant loose-leaf lettuce where you intend to grow corn, then harvest it before the corn has grown very large.

Popular Varieties. Basically there are four main types of lettuce: head lettuce, butterhead (also known as Boston or bibb lettuce), loose-leaf lettuce, and romaine (also called cos lettuce). Here are a few varieties that you might like to try:

Head lettuce

Great Lakes	90 days	Slow to bolt, stands up in warm weather; good quality heads, dark green fringed

Ithaca	72 days	Mild-heat resistant, usually does well in midsummer; heads firm
Oswego	70 days	Mild-heat resistant; slow bolting; heads firm even when immature (available from Seedway, Inc.)
Penlake	72 days	Early spring, uniform head, medium-green

Butterhead

Butter King	70 days	Heat-resistant; largest butterhead type
Buttercrunch	65 days	Heat-resistant; thick leaves
Summer Bibb	77 days	Heat-resistant; small dark-green leaves that don't look much like typical lettuce leaves
Big Boston	75 days	Cool-weather crop, broad leaves, smooth
Dark Green Boston	80 days	Cool-weather crop, thick leaves
Deer Tongue	80 days	Cool-weather crop, thick leaves
Bib	57 days	Cool-weather crop; small, dark-green leaves
Tom Thumb	65 days	Miniature head

Loose-leaf lettuce

Oakleaf	45 days	Heat-resistant; leaves shaped like oak leaves
Salad Bowl	50 days	Heat-resistant; crinkly leaves
Slobolt	45 days	Heat-resistant, slow-bolting, long-standing; crisp leaves
Black Seeded Simpson	46 days	Cool-weather crop; light green leaves, some crinkly
Grand Rapids	45 days	Cool-weather crop; easy to grow; crinkly leaves
Prizehead	45 days	Bronze-tinted leaves

Romaine

Paris Island Cos	76 days	Heat-resistant; firm heads 10 inches high
Paris White Cos	83 days	Heat-resistant; light-green leaves

Typical Problems. My lettuce keeps going to seed before it's big enough to eat.

Your lettuce is getting too much heat. You can solve this problem in any of several ways: (1) Plant earlier in the spring before hot weather sets in, or in late summer. (2) Shade your garden with lath or gauze. (3) Plant one of the varieties that are slow to bolt.

I always get poor heads and sometimes no heads at all.

You probably didn't thin out your plants enough. IPS beds let you plant a little closer than conventional gardens, but you must still thin a little to space out your heads.

My lettuce turns brown at the tips.

This is tip burn, due to hot weather. Again, you can prevent this by shading your garden as suggested above.

Harvesting. Head lettuce should be picked when the heads are nice and crisp. But, in general, the leaves of all types of lettuce remain edible at almost all stages; pick them as you need them.

Most IPS gardeners like to pick loose-leaf lettuce a leaf or two at a time. If you intend to do this leaf-picking, be sure to allow enough spacing (see above); otherwise, you're likely to wind up with bitter leaves.

A Lettuce Substitute for IPS Gardens—Endive

Endive makes a great lettuce substitute, but it's actually a member of the chicory family. You'll find it a little lacier than most lettuce and slightly bitter. Grow it just like you would lettuce. Endive is more heat- and cold-resistant than lettuce, and many gardeners find that they do best by planting it in the summer for fall or early winter harvesting. A good variety to try is Green Curled (90 days to maturity).

You generally need to "blanch" endive to lessen its bitterness and improve its flavor. Two or three weeks before you intend to start picking your endive, simply draw the outer leaves over the heart and center leaves until they come together at the top; then tie the bunched leaves together with string or rubber band. Be sure that the center leaves are dry when tied; otherwise they may rot.

Melons

Warm season crop. Rated fair to good for IPS gardens.

Melons take a lot of space, since they're determined to wander just about anywhere they please. Each vine stem may creep six to ten feet or more, and each plant will have several stems. Nevertheless, cantaloupes (also called muskmelons), watermelons, and other melons are the sentimental favorites of a lot of people; so if you insist on these fruits in a small garden, good luck. Actually, they're not that bad if you don't insist on watermelon (unless you plant the midget kind).

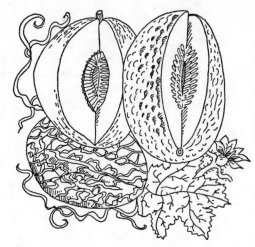

Planting. Melons are hot weather plants and can be planted about two weeks after the last frost. Plant seeds or seedlings 24 inches apart and train them up posts or other supports. (If you don't train them into the air, you'll be obliged to plant them 4 to 10 feet apart, because they'll spread out all over the place.)

Melons are heavy feeders and should be given a feeding of fish emulsion about every six weeks. (Apply according to the instructions on the bottle.) Also—this is crucial to their success—make sure that the ground never dries out while the plants are growing. Give them steady watering.

Crop Stretching. There's no reason at all why you can't grow cantaloupes and other small melons in quantity in a small portion of any good IPS garden. All you have to do is to grow the vines in the air. There are several ways:

(1) Sink a 6-foot post (preferably a 4 by 4) in the ground and stagger small crossbars on both sides up to the top. Tie the vines as they reach the crossbars, and support the fruit with cloth slings.

(2) Put up a construction-wire fence on one side of the garden and similarly tie the vines and fruit.

(3) Use a construction-wire island. Just form a circle of wire about 2 feet in diameter, and train three melon plants up this, tying the fruit as before.

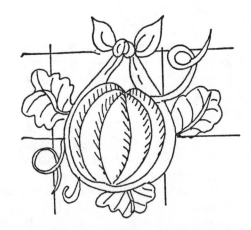

Popular Varieties.

Burpee Hybrid Cantaloupe	82 days	Fruit 7 inches long
Hearts of Gold	90 days	Medium-sized cantaloupe
Samson Hybrid	90 days	Deep-orange flesh cantaloupe
Gold Star	87 days	Early, heavy-yielding cantaloupe
Golden Beauty Casaba	120 days	White fruits, 6 to 8 inches across
Honey Dew	120 days	Green flesh, smooth ivory skin
Medium Persian	95 days	Large round, heavily netted melon without ridges
Minnesota Midget Muskmelon	60 days	Fruit 4 inches long
Golden Midget Watermelon	65 days	Midget; turns a golden color when ripe

Typical Problems. My melons taste bitter.

Usually this bitterness occurs when there is cold, wet weather during the ripening period. Melons need nice warm weather to be at their best.

I have blossom drop and no fruit setting.

Like the blossoms on cucumber vines, the first blossoms on melon vines are male. These will naturally drop. You should simply be patient until the female flowers come along; then you'll have small fruit developing.

Harvesting. Cantaloupes are ready to eat when the stems pull off easily—usually with a slight touch of the thumb. If they don't pull off easily, they should stay on the vine. You can also tell when they're ready because the skin begins to look like a corky net and the stem cracks a little all the way around.

For testing Persian melons, smell the blossom ends. If the smell is fruity and sweet, the melons are probably ripe.

Honeydew and casaba melons are ripe when the rinds have turned completely yellow.

For testing watermelons there's nothing like thumping them with your knuckle. They have a bonggg . . . sound (that is, a dull rather than a sharp sound). This is a great test for early morning; but once the watermelons get hot late in the day, it's pretty hard to tell whether or not they're good and ripe because the bong sound gives way to a dull thud. Another test is to look at the discolored spots where the melons touch the ground. If they're ready, these spots have turned from white to a pale yellow.

Mustard Greens

Cool season crop. Rated good for IPS gardens.

Mustard greens have long been a Southern favorite, and yet they've never really caught on in other sections of the country. There's no reason, however, why everybody can't enjoy this versatile vegetable. They're great as cooked greens and tremendous in salads. In addition (an important consideration for most gardeners), they grow to maturity fast.

Planting. In virtually every climate you can take out several crops of greens every year. Sow seed early in the spring, then again in late summer. If you live in an area of mild winters, plant again in the fall. Sow seeds ½ inch deep about 2 inches apart, and later thin the plants to 4 inches apart. (Be sure to cook up the tender thinned greens. They're delicious.)

Make sure that the plants get a continuous supply of water throughout the season.

Crop Stretching. Plant mustard greens in succession. Divide your mustard greens section into four subsections, planting each subsection three weeks apart.

You can also plant greens among tomato seedlings; the greens will be ready for harvesting before the tomato vines have grown large enough to shade them out.

Popular Varieties.

Florida Broad Leaf	43 days	Broad, smooth leaves
Southern Giant Curled	40 days	Bright green, fringed
Tendergreen	35 days	Rapid-growing, dark-green leaves, spinach flavor

Typical Problem. My mustard greens keep going to flower very early.

Mustard greens are a cool weather crop. If you keep having trouble with spring plantings, try planting in August for fall use.

Harvesting. Pick the leaves just before they mature. Be sure to keep the plants cut back to hold off flowering. After flowering, the leaves become tough and bitter.

Warm season crop. Rated fair for IPS gardens.   **Okra**

If you're from the South you probably know and love okra; but for some reason, except for an occasional brush in commercially prepared soups, people in the rest of the country often ignore okra, at least as a garden vegetable. If you'd like a delicious vegetable that will add flavor and body to soups and stews, you've got to include this one.

Unfortunately, the okra plant is too big to be a really good vegetable in our IPS gardens, but there is a dwarf variety that you can put in your flower borders, and it'll give you all the okra you'll need.

Planting. This is a warm weather plant with about the same requirements as corn. Plant only after the ground has warmed up. Soak the seeds overnight before planting, then plant them ½ to 1½ inches deep, about 8 inches apart. Thin the seedlings to 15 inches apart.

Give okra a feeding of fish emulsion at least once, six to eight weeks after planting. (Apply according to the directions on the bottle.)

Crop Stretching. Stick okra in odd corners of flowerbeds to use extra space that would ordinarily not be productive for vegetables.

Popular Varieties.

Clemson Spineless	56 days	Abundant producer, 4-foot plants
Dwarf Green Long Pod	52 days	2- to 2½-foot plants

Typical Problems. The buds keep dropping off, and no pods come.
This usually results from a lack of adequate moisture. Thus make sure that you water regularly during the growing season.
I planted my okra early in the spring, and the plants didn't do well for a long time.
Okra is a warm season crop. Don't plant until the soil has warmed.

Harvesting. Pick the pods young before they become too large—within a few days after the flower petals have fallen. Overripe pods, if left on the plants, will cause the plants to cease producing.

To freeze okra, cut the stems off the pods, blanch the pods in boiling water 2 to 3 minutes, cool, place in containers, and freeze.

Onions   *Cool season crop. Rated excellent for IPS gardens.*

Onions comprise a happy family of vegetables for gardeners and cooks. They're grown the world over and used as seasoning for meats, vegetables, and salads and as vegetables alone. Although they're mainly a cool weather crop, they'll do fine in moderately warm weather.

Planting. Onions can be grown from seeds, seedlings, or sets (small bulbs or roots).

Seeds should be scattered about 1 inch apart and covered with ½ inch of soil. As the plants rise, harvest the small onions so that the remaining plants are spaced about 2 or 3 inches apart; then let the mature bulbs develop.

Seedlings, purchased from a nursery, should be planted 1 inch apart and then thinned to 2 to 3 inches apart as they grow larger.

Sets, which are tiny bulbs, are probably the best way to grow onions, because they're good sized and easy to handle. Some varieties, such as red onions, however, can't be grown from sets but must be grown from seeds; and generally, in fact, the variety of onions that you'll find available as sets is pretty limited. In any case, plant sets 1 to 2 inches apart; then harvest green onions until the plants are spaced 2 to 3 inches apart, letting the remaining bulbs develop to maturity.

Seeds, seedlings, and sets should all be planted in early spring. In areas of mild winters they can be planted all winter long.

Onions need lots of moisture, especially during bulb formation (tops grow during cool weather, bulbs during warmer weather). A ·good general rule is to never allow the soil to dry out. Onions are also heavy feeders, but they do pretty well in our IPS soil without extra feeding.

Crop Stretching. Plant green onions between tomatoes, corn, eggplant, or other large plants, and harvest them before the later crops get big.

Popular Varieties. The two most popular kinds of onions are ordinary bulbing onions and bunching onions. Bunching onions are usually called green onions (or scallions).

The green onions listed below are varieties especially intended to be harvested as green onions. However, dry bulb onions can be harvested as small green onions just twenty to thirty days after planting; only if you leave them in the ground for the length of time noted will they become bulb onions.

Green onions

Evergreen Long White Bunching	120 days	Long, slender white stalks
White Spanish Green Bunching	100 days	Vigorous grower, mild flavor

Dry bulb onions

Yellow Sweet Spanish	115 days	Big yellow, globe-shaped
Early Yellow Globe	100 days	Deep yellow, globe-shaped
Southport Yellow Globe	115 days	Yellow, deep globular
Yellow Bermuda	95 days	Yellow, mild-flavored
White Sweet Spanish	110 days	White, round, large
Southport Red Globe	110 days	Dark red, globe-shaped

Typical Problem. My onions didn't get very big.
You probably let the soil dry out during bulb enlargement. Make sure that you water regularly.

Harvesting. When the tops of ordinary bulb onions begin to dry and yellow, bend them over to a nearly horizontal position on the ground, or break them off. This will divert all growing energy to the bulbs. When all the tops are dead, dig the bulbs up and let them dry on top of the ground for a few days; then store them in a dry, frost-free place indefinitely.

Green onions can be harvested as needed. But you should recognize that they don't keep long after harvesting, even with refrigeration.

Cool season crop. Rated good to excellent for IPS gardens. **Peas**
Peas are nearly always a star performer in the garden. They come up

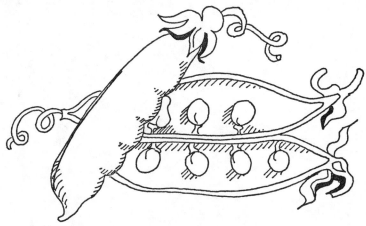

right away, bloom fast, and produce lots of food within 60 to 80 days. Peas are a cool season crop, thriving in soil and air filled with cool moisture. Although they'll continue growing and producing when the days become somewhat warmer and longer, they do not do well in hot dry weather.

Planting. Pea plants grow only from seeds planted directly in the bed where they're going to remain. Plant the seeds in the spring as soon as the ground can be worked, sowing them 2 inches deep, 2 inches apart. Use successive plantings, five to ten days apart, for a continuous crop.

Crop Stretching. Peas grow either as bushes or as vines. The vines can—and should—be trained in the air, and we can do this any number of ways:

1. Place chicken wire fence along the north side of your garden, and train your vines on it.

2. Sink a 4-foot post (preferably a 2 by 2) in the ground with a 1-foot cross nailed to the top. Run pea vines (about 12 plants) up strings stretched from the ground to the cross. You can station several of these crosses around the garden.

3. Make a construction wire island: form a circle of wire about 2 feet in diameter and 5 feet high and plant and train pea vines inside it. When harvest time comes, you can pick the pods through the wires.

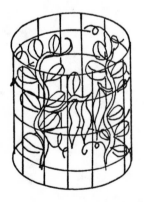 

Popular Varieties. The common green peas, also called garden peas or English peas, are grown for their edible seeds; they grow as vines or bushes. Peas grown for their edible pods, popular in Oriental cooking, are known as Chinese snow peas or sugar peas and grow as vines.

Bush green peas

Alaska	55 days	Bush 18-24 inches tall; plump green pods, very early
Burpee's Blue Bantam	64 days	Bush 15-18 inches tall; sweet
Progress No. 9	60 days	Bush 20 inches tall; early
Little Marvel	63 days	Bush 18 inches tall; pods 3 inches long

Vine green peas

Alderman	74 days	Vine 4½-6 feet tall, extra sweet
Wando	68 days	Vine 2½ feet tall, heat tolerant
Freezonian	63 days	Vine 2½ feet tall, good for freezing

Edible-pod peas

Burpee's Sweetpod	68 days	Vine 4 feet tall, thick pods
Dwarf Gray Sugar	65 days	Vine 2-2½ feet tall, early

Typical Problems. My vines are lush and bushy but produce few peas.
To start them producing, simply pinch back the growing tips of the various stems thereby thinning out the vine a little.
My pea pods are hard when I pick them.
You're letting them stay on the vines too long. Pick them regularly.
My peas aren't growing well; the tips of the leaves seem to be dying.
Peas need lots of water when the weather is warm and the atmosphere dry. If the days are extremely hot, there's not much you can do; you *must* grow peas in cool weather.

Harvesting. Pick off all the pods as they mature in order to keep the plants producing vigorously. It is best to harvest only in the morning; this seems to preserve their flavor. After picking, shell them and store them in the refrigerator as soon as possible.
For freezing peas, shell them, blanch the seeds in boiling water about 3 minutes, cool, place in containers, and freeze.

Peppers   *Warm season crop. Rated excellent for IPS gardens.*

Pepper plants are very pretty. It's not the flowers that make them so attractive, however; it's the fruit and foliage, and they make great ornamentals.

Peppers originally came to the attention of the Western world when explorers landing in the New World tasted the native chili and mistook it for the spice "pepper," one of the trading spices from the Orient. This New World "pepper," however, tasted only vaguely like the East Indian pepper that they were looking for. In point of fact, the various sweet and hot peppers native to the New World are related to the tomato and eggplant.

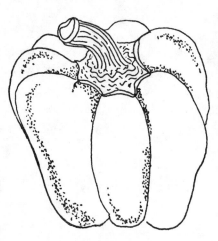

Planting. Peppers are classified as hot weather plants; thus they like temperatures above 60° F. On the other hand, they also like temperatures below 90° F. Anywhere out of this temperature range from 60° to 90° seems to keep the fruit from setting.

You can start peppers either from seeds or from plants purchased from your local nursery. If you're going to use seeds, you should start them indoors in peat pots—two to four seeds ½ inch deep in each pot— about ten weeks before you intend to set the plants out.

In your garden bed space the seedlings 14 inches apart.

Peppers need lots of regular watering. They are also heavy feeders, and you should give them a feeding of fish emulsion about the time that the first blossoms open. (Apply according to the instructions on the bottle.)

Popular Varieties. There are a lot of different kinds of peppers—all shapes and sizes and colors—but generally the most common can be divided into two classes: sweet and hot. The sweet we know as bell peppers.

Sweet peppers

Bell Boy Hybrid	75 days	Block-shaped
Burpee's Fordhook	65 days	Tender fruit 3-3½ inches in diameter
California Wonder	75 days	Good stuffing pepper

Midway	72 days	Big crop under adverse weather conditions
Morgold	72 days	Early, big-fruited
Keystone Resistant Giant	80 days	Vigorous plant, thick-fleshed fruit
Yolo Wonder	70 days	Thick-fleshed fruit, dark green turning red

Hot peppers

Long Red Cayenne	72 days	5 inches long, often curled, easy to dry
Anaheim M	77 days	Long tapered, thick-fleshed
Yellow Wax Hungarian	70 days	Yellow changing to red
Large Cherry	69 days	Flattened fruit, 1½ inches across

A novelty to try

Sweet Banana	60 days	Banana-shaped, 8 inches long, light yellow in color

Typical Problem. The blossoms dropped off, and I stopped getting fruit.

This could be the result of a couple of things. The night temperatures may have become too hot or too cold; if so, there's not much you can do. Or you may not be picking the ripe peppers regularly; pepper plants usually won't continue producing more blossoms when the plants have all the fruit they can handle.

Harvesting. Pick bell peppers when they are firm and crisp. Most people believe that they have a better flavor when picked green, not red.

Let hot peppers completely ripen on the vine.

For freezing, first dice or slice them and then freeze them one hour in an uncovered pan. Then put the pieces in small bags and return to the freezer.

Radishes

Cool season crop. Rated excellent for IPS gardens.

The radish is a quick-maturing, here-today and gone-tomorrow plant. Some varieties of radish mature in as few as 22 days; others average about a month—which is fast for most vegetables. They're also ridiculously easy to grow; give anyone a package of radish seeds, and you make him an instant gardener.

Planting. Just pop your radish seeds in the ground as soon as it can be worked; after that, sow more seeds every week or so to assure a continuous crop. It is best to plant only what you can eat in a week or so; then you won't get overloaded with radishes. Because radishes are a cool weather crop, halt the sowing in early summer and then resume about a month before the first frost.

The seeds should be scattered about 1 inch apart, ½ inch deep.

Crop Stretching. Radishes can be sown early in places where you will be planting such later crops as corn and tomatoes. Because of the speed with which radishes grow, you can plant them between any vegetables that require a 4- or 5-inch spacing; the radishes will be harvested before the main crops get very big.

Popular Varieties. There are two main kinds of radishes: the ordinary ones (though of many shapes and hues), which are small and quick-maturing; and the winter ones, which are usually large and require cool weather at the end of their growing season. The winter varieties should be sown in midsummer. Although both the skin and flesh of ordinary radishes are edible, the skin of winter radishes should be peeled to reveal the edible white flesh.

Ordinary radishes

Cherry Belle	22 days	Round cherry-sized, smooth, red
French Breakfast	23 days	Red-white tip, oblong to olive-shaped, tops short
Sparkler	25 days	Red top, lower third white; almost round, crisp
Burpee White	25 days	White, nearly round
White Icicle	28 days	White, 5 inches long

Winter radishes

White Chinese	60 days	Pure white, 6-8 inches long
China Rose	52 days	7 inches by 2 inches; hot, crisp
Round Black Spanish	55 days	Smooth, round, deep-black skin

A novelty to try

Sakurajima Radish   70 days   Size of a watermelon, often
                                                  weighing 15 pounds

Typical Problems. I get lots of leaves but no radish bottoms.
You sowed the seeds too close together. Thin the plants to at least 1 inch apart.
My radishes taste so hot I can hardly eat them.
Sometimes this happens when the soil becomes hot and dries out. Keep watering regularly.

Harvesting. Pick radishes when they're still fairly small and young (pull up a couple to see). They'll be tender, succulent, and full of flavor at this stage. Later on they'll be somewhat pithy.

Rhubarb

Cool season crop. Rated fair for IPS gardens.
If you like big-leaved plants, you'll love this one. It looks almost like a tropical growing in your garden, and it compares favorably with any of the broad-leaved plants grown primarily as ornamentals. Rhubarb, however, is a perennial, like asparagus, and will spread out and take up an awful lot of space. It's therefore not the best thing for IPS gardens. That shouldn't rule it out, though, because it'll do very well in its own separate bed or especially in your flower beds, where it'll look tremendous.

Planting. Rhubarb doesn't do well in most subtropical regions of the United States because it needs a winter dormant period. On the other hand, I grew it well at one time in San Jose, California, so I know that it can handle fairly mild winters.

You should purchase root crowns from your nursery and plant them 12 inches apart in the spring or fall (36 inches apart if you want giant plants). Dig holes and set the plants in so that the tops of the roots stand 3 or 4 inches below ground level; cover with soil. Wait two years after planting before you begin to pull stalks for eating. From then on you'll have ample yield for the next eight or nine years.

Water rhubarb regularly and deep, and give the plants a feeding of fish emulsion once or twice a year (apply according to the instructions on the bottle).

Crop Stretching. Put rhubarb in odd flower bed space not suited for other vegetables.

Popular Varieties.

MacDonald	Brilliant red stalks
Valentine	Deep-red stalks
Victoria	Green rhubarb stalks

Typical Problems. Practically none.

Harvesting. Select the larger outside stalks; grasp them firmly near the base and snap them off. Use only the stalks for eating; discard the dark green leaves, which are poisonous.

For freezing rhubarb, wash the stalks, cut them in ¾-inch slices, put in containers, and freeze.

Spinach   *Cool season crop. Rated fair to good for IPS gardens.*

Spinach is one of those on-again, off-again vegetables. I live in one of those areas where it may be cool in March and April and 90° a few weeks later in May. That's what you might call a spinach grower's nightmare, because spinach must have cool weather, or else. Give it long days and hot temperatures, and all of a sudden it's gone to seed.

Planting. Spinach grows best from seeds, set directly in the ground where they're to grow. Sow the seeds in early spring and again in late summer, placing them about ½ inch deep and 2 inches apart. Thin the seedlings to about 6 inches apart. For a long crop, make successive plantings ten days apart.

Spinach is a heavy feeder, so give the plants a feeding of fish emulsion about halfway through the season. (Apply according to the directions on the bottle.)

Crop Stretching. You can harvest your early spinach in the late spring and then plant beans. Later, when it cools off, you can follow the beans with another planting of spinach for a fall crop.

Popular Varieties.

Long Standing Bloomsdale	48 days	Heavy yielder, crinkly; remains in rosette stage for a long time without bolting
America	50 days	Dark green, slow-bolting
Winter Bloomsdale	45 days	Smooth, dark-green leaves; will winter over from a fal sowing
Hybrid No. 7	42 days	Upright, semi-savoy type; good for fall and winter

Typical Problem. My spinach flowers every spring before I get a good crop.

The problem is that spinach tends to flower (bolt) quickly, especially as the days get longer and the temperatures a little higher. The only solution is to grow a variety, like Bloomsdale Long Standing, that is slow to bolt. Or, if you live in an area of mild winters, plant in late summer or in the fall for a late crop.

Harvesting. Harvest the outer leaves when the plants are full size (when the outer leaves are at least 3 inches long). If you pick just the outer leaves, the inner ones will become the next crop.

For freezing spinach, pick the tender leaves only, blanch them in boiling water 1½ minutes, cool, put in containers, and freeze.

A Spinach Substitute for IPS Gardens—New Zealand Spinach. New Zealand spinach is not a true spinach, but a succulent plant from New Zealand that resembles spinach in appearance and is highly heat- and drought-resistant. For this reason you can grow it all summer long when spinach would be impossible.

New Zealand spinach is a low-growing, ground-cover type plant that spreads 3 to 4 feet across.

Seeds can be started indoors or outdoors. Indoors, sow them in peat pots 1 inch deep and then transplant the seedlings to the garden after the last frost. Outdoors, simply sow the seeds 1 inch deep, about 8 inches apart.

Harvest New Zealand spinach by cutting the young tender stems when you need them.

Squash   *Warm season crop. Rated good for IPS gardens.*

Traditional gardeners grow both summer squash and winter squash: summer squash, harvested and cooked in summer while immature and soft-skinned, will not store for long; winter squash, which is left on the vines until the shells are thoroughly hardened and leaves turn brown, stores well for fall and winter use. IPS gardeners should prefer summer squash because it produces smaller fruit with thinner skins, grows usually as bushy compact plants, and doesn't take up much space.

Winter squash has runner-type vines that can require lots of space. Nevertheless, although IPS gardeners probably should stick to summer squash, they can grow the vines of winter squash in the air as we do cucumbers. The heavy fruits, though, must be tied up with cloth supports.

Planting. Squash is extremely easy to grow, but it's a heat lover and shouldn't be set outdoors until nighttime temperatures regularly stay above 55° F.

Use seeds or seedlings purchased from a nursery. Plant seeds 1 inch deep, 18 inches apart. Set seedlings 18 inches apart.

Crop Stretching. Small-fruited winter squash can be trained up in the air on the same kind of structures used for cucumbers. Be sure to support the fruit with cloth slings.

Popular Varieties. Among the varieties of summer squash zucchini is a wonder, because so many things can be done with it: you can stuff it, fry it, bake it in a casserole, or cut it up for salads. Generally you'll find two or three zucchini plants enough because the plants are so prolific. I swear that you can find it in bloom one morning, then come back two days later and pick a full-blown zucchini. You should also try some of the other summer varieties. As I said, most winter varieties are too big for IPS gardens, but I'm listing one that you might try.

Summer squash

Burpee Hybrid Zucchini	50 days	Plant medium-sized, bushlike, and compact; fruit shiny and medium-green
Cocozelle Bush	60 days	Cylindrical dark-green fruit
Early Golden Summer Crookneck	53 days	Bright yellow meaty fruit shaped like a gourd
Early Prolific Straightneck	50 days	Bushlike plant; fruit long and yellow
Early White Bush	54 days	Round fruit with scalloped edges, pale green to creamy white

Winter squash

Gold Nugget	85 days	Bush-type plant; fruit bright orange and oval

Typical Problem. My zucchini plants start out each year producing some small squash that rot before they get very big.
Some female flowers on the plant bloomed before there were male flowers around to pollinate them. These unpollinated flowers result in small fruits that rot. Just wait and you'll get plenty of zucchini that will grow to full size.

Harvesting. Pick summer squash when it's fairly young and small. It's tender and delicious then. Usually summer squash is too old for eating when the thumbnail doesn't readily pierce the skin with little pressure.
Let winter squash mature fully on the vine until its skin is very hard.
Both summer and winter squash can be frozen, but winter squash must first be peeled. Cut the squash into small pieces, blanch the pieces in boiling water 1½ minutes, cool, place in containers, and freeze.

Swiss Chard   *Cool season crop. Rated good for IPS gardens.*

If you've tried spinach and failed or are just tired of fighting its special weather requirements, then you'll want to grow Swiss chard, for it can take summer temperatures that would make spinach bolt to seed. Chard, a member of the beet family, but without the bulbous root, has delicious big crinkly leaves and delicious white stalks. That's a double dividend. The leaves are cooked like spinach or other greens. The stalks are cooked and served like asparagus.

Planting. In cold winter areas, plant seeds in the spring about two or three weeks before the final frost; in areas where winter temperatures stay above 25° F., plant in the fall for harvesting the next year. In fact, in regions of very mild climates you can plant almost any time of the year.

In planting chard, we make an exception to one of our IPS rules. Unlike other vegetables in the IPS garden, chard must be planted in rows. The seeds should not be broadcast. Make rows about 12 inches apart, and sow seeds in these rows ½ inch deep and about 4 inches apart. When the seedlings come up, thin them to at least 8 inches apart.

Crop Stretching. Plant Swiss chard in spaces that will later contain corn, tomatoes, and other heat lovers.

Popular Varieties.

Fordhook Giant	60 days	Dark-green leaves, much curled
Burpee's Rhubarb Chard	60 days	Wine-red leaves resembling rhubarb

Typical Problems. Almost none.

Harvesting. There are two ways to harvest Swiss chard. Every few days you can cut the outer leaves from the plant while it continues growing. (Don't let old and tough leaves remain on the plant, or the plant will stop producing fresh leaves.) Or you can also cut off the whole plant a couple of inches above the root crown, and the plant will produce new leaves.

Warm season crop. Excellent for IPS gardens.   **Tomatoes**

The tomato is one of those strange vegetables that seem to grow well in spite of what people do to it. One of my neighbors plants a few tomato plants in the backyard, then barely waters or weeds them, yet they always seem to come out great. I have another neighbor, on the other hand, who takes meticulous care of his tomato plants, selects the varieties carefully, plants them at the right time, then sprays and feeds them religiously. His crops turn out great too—which leads me to believe that it's pretty hard to go very far wrong growing tomatoes. Temperature seems to be the crucial factor. As warm-weather plants, tomato seedlings should not be set out in the garden until nighttime temperatures begin staying above 58° F.

Planting. You can start your tomatoes from seeds or buy them as seedlings. Buying seedlings is the easiest way, and the one I use. You'll generally have to grow from seed, however, if you want a wide choice of varieties.

To start from seeds, plant them ½ inch deep in compressed peat pots; then after the weather outdoors has warmed up, plant the pots with the seedlings in your IPS beds 18 inches apart.

There are a couple of rules that you should follow when transplanting seedlings. If you have a bushy plant (which is preferable to a long lean one), bury it so that half to three-quarters of the stem as well as the root ball is below the soil level; roots will form along the buried stem. For really long-stemmed plants, you still want to get half to three-quarters of the stem underground, but you want to be careful not to place the root ball too deep. Thus, in a shallow hole, you should put the root ball almost on its side so that the stem is almost horizontal, or at least not vertical; then you gradually bend the stem so that only the bushy part appears upright above ground level.

Tomatoes generally are deep-rooted, often going six feet deep or more. The plants should get plenty of moisture during the growing season. Over-watering, however, can stimulate too much leaf growth and cause blossoms to drop. Too much shade or too much nitrogen fertilizer can also cut down blossoming. Despite these apparent problems, tomatoes seem easy to grow.

If you have tomato diseases around (ask your nurseryman), you can avoid them by looking for the letters V, F, and N on the instructions

93

accompanying your seeds or seedlings. The letters stand for varieties resistant to verticillium, fusarium, and nematode, major tomato diseases.

Tomatoes are heavy feeders, but in an IPS bed it usually isn't necessary to give them an extra feeding during the season.

Crop Stretching. There are several ways to adapt tomato plants to an IPS garden:

1. Make a fence of chicken wire stretched between two 5- or 6-foot posts (preferably 2 by 2s). As the plants grow, cut back enough foliage to make each plant easy to tie to the wires, but leave as many stems as possible—say, two to six. (This way you'll get more fruit.)

2. Make a lath framework or trellis for each plant. Pinch off all but two or four main stems and tie them to the frame.

3. The best thing for IPS gardens is to make a circular tomato cage from a 5-foot length of construction wire. (That's the kind used for concrete reinforcing, with a 6-inch mesh.) Just circle each plant in your garden with the wire, and tie the ends of the wire together. You don't have to cut off any plant stems, but you'll probably have to tie the stems to the wire. This tomato cage will give you an extremely productive bushy tomato factory.

Popular Varieties. You've got a lot of choices of tomatoes, so let's divide the varieties into early, midseason, and late; large fruit, small fruit, and midgets; yellows and other variations.

The early varieties set fruit at lower temperatures than later maturing plants; you get tomatoes much earlier in the season.

Early

Burpee's Big Early Hybrid	62 days	Big fruit, prolific producer
Spring Giant Hybrid	65 days	Scarlet fruit, heavy producer
Fireball	65 days	Medium-sized fruit
New Yorker	64 days	Medium-sized fruit, mild flavor

Midseason and late

Heinz 1350	75 days	Slightly flattened fruit, heavy yielding
Glamour	80 days	Crack-resistant
Marglobe	73 days	Medium-large fruit, vigorous grower

Large fruit

Burpee's Big Boy	78 days	Fruit often weighing a pound, heavy producer
Rutgers	72 days	Vigorous vines
Ponderosa	88 days	Enormous scarlet fruit, low acid

Small fruit

Red Cherry	72 days	Fruit about 7/8 inch across
Basket Pat	76 days	Bite-sized tomatoes

Midget

Tiny Tim	55 days	Plants only 15 inches tall

Yellow

Sunray	72 days	Orange-yellow fruit
Burpee's Jubilee	72 days	Golden orange fruit, good yields

Novelties to try

Yellow Pear	70 days	Pear-shaped yellow fruit
Yellow Plum	70 days	Plum-shaped yellow fruit, sweet

Typical Problems. I planted in the spring, and the plants took forever to start growing.

Remember that tomatoes are a warm season plant. They'll just sit there looking unhappy if you put them out while it's still too cold. Nighttime temperatures should be above 58° at least. In fact, tomatoes grow best in a fairly narrow temperature range—70° to 75° at night and 80° to 90° during the day.

My tomato blossoms keep dropping off instead of producing fruit.

This happens when the night temperatures go much below 58°. The problem corrects itself when the nights become warmer. Excess heat can cause the same problem.

My tomato plants look great; they're nice and bushy; but they're just not producing any tomatoes.

This could happen because they're getting too much shade or too much water or because it's too hot at night. Try pinching off the terminal shoots, and cut down on the water that you're giving your plants.

Harvesting. Tomatoes are best harvested when they have reached their full color. But they may also be picked when showing only a tinge of red, then stored in a warm, dark place to ripen.

Tomato puree can be frozen. Douse the tomatoes in boiling water for a few seconds so that you can skin them easily; remove the seeds if you wish; then puree the skinned tomatoes in a blender, package the puree, and freeze.

Turnips and Rutabagas

Cool season crops. Rated good for IPS gardens.

Turnips and rutabagas aren't grown nearly so often in gardens as are other kinds of root crops such as carrots and beets, but they really have their own distinctive flavor and a very enthusiastic group of fans. The roots of both plants look alike, both having purplish tops; but turnips have white flesh and are about two inches across, and rutabagas have either white or yellow flesh and are about four or five inches across. Also the leaves of turnips are edible as cooked greens; the leaves of rutabagas are not.

Planting. Turnips and rutabagas are both cool season vegetables and should be planted as early in the spring as the ground can be worked. Sow the seeds 1/8 to 1/4 inch deep, about 1 inch apart; and in stages thin the resultant seedlings to 2 inches apart for turnips, 6 inches apart for rutabagas.

Turnips can also be planted in spring and midsummer in the cooler northern parts of the country. Where winters are frost-free and mild, they can be planted in the fall. Turnips mature in about 35 to 60 days, rutabagas in about 90.

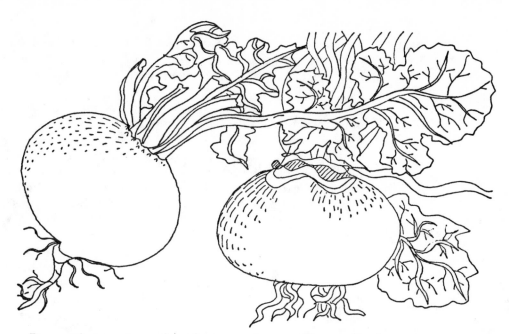

Be sure that turnips and rutabagas receive a steady supply of water to maturity.

Crop Stretching. Plant turnips and rutabagas between cabbages.

Popular Varieties.

Turnip

Early Purple Top Milan	45 days	Flattened roots, 3-4 inches across
Tokyo Cross	35 days	Smooth, pure white
Just Right Hybrid	60 days	Fine flavor, white

Rutabaga

Improved American Purple Top	88 days	Roots 5-7 inches across

Typical Problems. Practically none.

Harvesting. Harvest turnip roots when they are 2 to 4 inches in diameter and before they get pithy. For turnip greens, harvest the leaves when they are young and tender.

Harvest rutabagas when the roots are about 3 to 5 inches in diameter.

For freezing turnips and rutabagas, peel the roots, cut them into cubes, blanch them in boiling water 1 to 2 minutes, cool them, place them in containers, and freeze.

Herbs

Herbs are fun to grow and great for kitchen use, and many gardeners insist that they have beneficial effects in the garden; in Chapters 7 and 8 we'll discuss some of the good effects.

For the kitchen, you can always use herbs fresh; just pick pieces as you need them. You can also dry them for storage, but they should be dried quickly and in the dark, in order to preserve their best flavor. You do this by placing them on a cookie sheet and placing them in the oven for 2 to 3 hours at the lowest possible heat setting. The oven door should be left slightly ajar (but without the light on). Store the dried herbs in glass or metal containers that can be closed tightly to preserve the flavor.

Now here are a few herbs that you'll want to try.

Basil. Most Italian cooks would be lost without sweet basil to flavor pasta and other Italian dishes. It's also great for almost any other kind of cooking. The plant is an annual with light-green foliage that grows 1 to 2 feet high. It also comes in a bush form.

Basil will make an attractive plant set in a sunny corner of your flower beds or stuck into a few odd corners of your IPS garden. Simply sow the seeds about 2 inches apart after the last frost. To harvest basil, cut the stems regularly—the more you cut the more they grow. When the plants flower, cut them about 6 inches from the ground, dry them, and then strip the leaves and flowers and store these in jars.

Chives. Chives are a gourmet's delight. You can buy pots of chives from a nursery and separate them. Plant a clump in your IPS garden, or stuff them in an odd corner of a flower bed. (They prefer full sun but will tolerate filtered shade.) When you need some leaves, just clip off what you need.

Dill. I can well remember my mother using dill to make pickles many years ago, and its slightly bitter taste and unusual fragrance have always held a fascination for me. Sometimes the "weeds" or stems are used to flavor salads (especially Greek salads) and to flavor fish and lamb. In the past it's been used as a drug, and even today many people believe that dill has curative powers. The plant itself grows 4 feet high, with flowers in clusters.

Sow dill seeds in spring or late summer in a sunny area, and thin the young plants to about 10 inches apart. Harvest the leaves when you need them. Harvest the seeds from the flower beds when they begin to turn brown.

Garlic. Garlic is not really an herb, but a relative of the onion. It is strong medicine, and many gardeners insist that the plant (and its extracts) can be used to control a wide range of insects. (See Chapter 8.) There are two types available—regular garlic bulbs, which contain a number of small cloves, and elephant garlic. Elephant garlic has the flavor of regular garlic, but none of its strong pungency. You can, for instance, slice elephant cloves right into salads. Elephant garlic can be ordered from the Burgess Seed and Plant Company or the Nichols Garden Nursery. (See the appendix for addresses.)

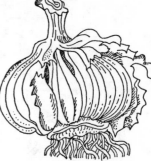

Plant garlic cloves 1 to 1½ inches deep, 2 inches apart, base down, in an area of full sun. To harvest, dig the roots up when the tops fall over.

Marjoram. Throughout history, sweet marjoram was thought to have medicinal uses. That may be all past, but still we love this herb for cooking—as a seasoning for zucchini, as a wonderful flavoring for Italian dishes, and as an enrichment for many other foods too. Sweet marjoram is a bushy plant that grows 1 to 2 feet high.

Start marjoram seeds indoors in winter; then after the last frost set the small plants in sunny areas in your garden. Harvest the leaves and stem tips at any time and use them fresh. (New leaves and stems will appear after the cuttings.) Or pick the leaves just before blossoming, dry and store them.

Mint. Everybody should have a little mint planted around somewhere—to use for iced tea, lamb dishes, and many other foods and drinks. You can grow spearmint, orange mint, peppermint, and thirty or more other flavors. The distinctive flavors in all the mints come from the oils produced within the plants. Spearmint is probably the favorite of most gardeners; it grows from 1 to 2 feet high, producing clusters of flowers on spikes. Orange mint grows to about the same height and has a subtle taste and smell comparable to that of oranges. Peppermint grows to 3 feet, producing spikes of tiny purple flowers.

To start mint, plant roots or runners in the spring, or buy a few plants from a nursery. It wants plenty of water, prefers full sun, but will tolerate partial shade. To harvest, simply cut a few sprigs whenever you need them; the more often you cut, the better the plants grow. You can also dry the leaves for storage.

Oregano. Sometimes called wild marjoram, oregano (or origanum) has been an essential seasoning in Latin cooking since ancient times and today is found in many Italian, Spanish, and Mexican dishes. The plant is a hardy perennial shrub growing 2½ feet tall.

Start oregano from seeds, or buy small plants from a nursery. Because oregano starts slowly, some gardeners like to begin seeds indoors in winter and transplant the seedlings later to their gardens after the last frost. To harvest, pick the leaves as you need them. You can also dry the leaves and store them for later use.

Parsley. Parsley is an old favorite that can garnish almost anything and is especially good in salads. There are several kinds shown in the seed catalogs: Banquet (76 days) has fine, tightly curled leaves and is ideal for garnishing. Perfection (75 days) is early and vigorous, producing finely curled leaves. Plain Italian Dark Green (78 days) has flat leaves, like celery leaves, that have a strong flavor and are excellent for salads. Hamburg (90 days) has a root that can be boiled and served like parsnips. Extra Curled Dwarf (85 days) has compact plants, producing fine leaves. Plain or Single (72 days) has plain dark-green, deeply cut, flat leaves that have a rich fine flavor.

Sow parsley seeds outdoors in spring or summer. Soak the seeds in warm water twenty-four hours before planting to hurry them along, since they're slow to germinate. Sow them 1 to 2 inches apart, and then thin the seedlings to 8 to 10 inches apart. To harvest, pick mature leaves whenever you need them.

Rosemary. Rosemary is a great seasoning for veal, lamb, and fish and is used in many sauces and breadings. As a plant, it looks like an evergreen shrub, and it can grow to 6 feet tall. Fortunately, there's also a dwarf form, only 2 feet tall. You can use rosemary in your IPS garden if you keep it trimmed back; otherwise, plant it in a flower bed in a sunny spot where it won't spread out to crowd your other plants.

You can propagate rosemary from cuttings taken from a growing plant, or you can buy small plants from a nursery. To harvest, just cut off leaves whenever you need them.

Sage. Sage is good in all kinds of dressings and stuffings, for pork as well as for poultry; and it's often used in making sausage or pâté. The plant is a gray-leaved perennial, growing 1 to 2 feet tall, and there are many varieties; Golden Leaf, Red Tricolor, Vatican Dwarf, and others.

You can grow sage from cuttings taken from existent plants; you can plant seeds; or you can buy small plants from a nursery. If you use seeds, plant them indoors in the winter and later transplant the seedlings. Give sage full sun. To harvest, pick the leaves during the growing season before blossoming. Cut the plant back to the ground as soon as it's stopped blooming; the plant will renew the next year.

Savory. Savory was one of the earliest of cultivated medicinal herbs. Today we use it mainly in cooking beans, other vegetables, and soups and in preparing seasoned salads. There are two kinds, summer savory and winter savory. Summer savory, which is the most popular, is an annual that grows 18 inches high. Winter savory is a perennial, also growing to about 18 inches.

Start summer savory from seed planted in the place where you want it to grow. Start winter savory from cuttings taken from existing plants, or buy plants from a nursery. To harvest, take leaves during the growing season. Cut back winter savory to the ground as soon as it stops blooming; it will arise again the next season.

Tarragon. Tarragon is a seasoning for fish, salad dressings, stews, sauces, vegetables, and many other things. Tarragon is a perennial that grows to about 2 feet. Once started, it's good for about two years.

You can grow tarragon from cuttings taken from existing plants, but most gardeners buy small plants from a nursery. To harvest, cut the leaves during the growing season before blooming. Dry leaves for preserving.

Thyme. There are so many thymes available that you hardly know which one to grow first; there are lemon thyme, caraway thyme, golden thyme, French thyme, and more. As the names imply, lemon thyme has a lemon scent, caraway a caraway scent. All varieties make good seasonings for vegetables and meat sauces. The plants grow 8 to 12 inches tall.

You can sow seeds indoors in the winter and later transplant the seedlings outside; you can start plants from cuttings taken from existing plants; or you can buy small plants from a nursery. Plant tarragon in full sun, 8 to 12 inches apart. Replant every three years. To harvest, cut the plants when in full bloom. After blooming, cut the plants back to the ground; they will arise again the following year.

And that's our roundup on herbs. You can buy the plants or seeds from nurseries, grocery stores, and a lot of variety stores. The most complete selection of herbs that I've ever seen offered is carried by Nichols Garden Nursery (the address is in the appendix). It offers ten varieties of thyme, for instance. You can get them by mail.

So now you're well started on which vegetables can be grown in your garden. As you can see, there's really a wide selection; and as you get more experience and really become an avid gardener, you'll want to hunt through the seed catalogs, looking for different or unusual varieties that you've never tried before. And you can experiment to see just how much you can really grow in the space that you have available. That's half the fun of gardening; and, from now on, the more vegetables that you take out of your own garden the more the vegetable urge will get you. After that, there's just no stopping.

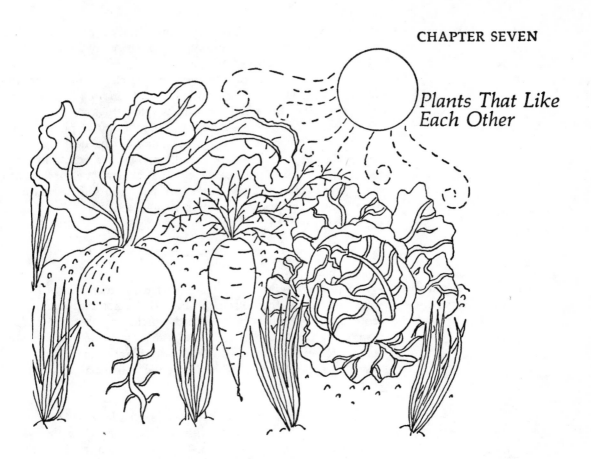

CHAPTER SEVEN

Plants That Like Each Other

Ecology has become a household word in America in the past few years, and the kind of gardening that we're recommending in this book is based on ecological principles—maintaining the balance of nature and restoring to the earth what we take from it. We are practicing applied ecology. An important part of this effort is something called companion planting, which rests on the idea that certain species of plants aid each other by their mere presence together or, conversely, that certain species do poorly when living together.

There is much evidence that plant relationships and disrelationships are extremely important. In the early 1900s Rudolf Steiner and his followers in Europe developed and explored the companion plant concept. Later, Richard Gregg carried on a great deal of field observation in New York; and still later, E.E. Pfeiffer developed what is called crystalization to determine the relationships between plants.

It is now known from other research that all plants give off chemicals called root diffusates, which affect other plants in various ways. Moreover, the aromas given off by some of the herbs repel or attract certain types of insects. Which ones do what? It's really pretty hard to tell. This is an area intertwined with old wives tales and some facts. Nevertheless, there is a great deal of truth concerning the compatibility of plants, and the information should help make our gardens healthier and more vigorous; and that, after all, is what we want. In this chapter, I'll give you some of the general beliefs about particular plants, and you can experiment yourself to find out what works best for you in your own garden.

Companion Vegetables

Asparagus. Some gardeners find that asparagus likes tomatoes and makes them grow profusely. It's not that simple, of course, but scientists have indeed isolated a substance called asparagin which seems to exert a good influence on tomato plants. Many gardeners thus like to plant tomatoes in the asparagus bed after they've harvested the asparagus in the spring.

Beans. Beans seem very compatible. Gardeners have found that they do pretty well with beets, carrots, cauliflower, cucumbers, corn, and radishes. They don't seem to like onions, garlic, and other members of the onion family; planted too close together, both beans and onions tend to be stunted in their growth.

Beets. Beets seem to do well with almost everything that we grow in our IPS garden—except pole beans. Here they're set back. They do especially well with lettuce, cabbage, onions, and even bush beans. Why there's a difference in compatibility toward the different bean varieties, pole and bush, has not been adequately explained, but apparently the chemistry is different.

Broccoli. Broccoli seems to do well near all the smelly kinds of herbs and onions.

Brussels Sprouts. Brussels sprouts, like broccoli and all other members of the cabbage family, are influenced by aromatic herbs and seem to be stimulated by close planting with almost any of them.

Cabbage. Cabbage and all other members of the cabbage family have undergone a rather specialized development. Cabbage itself, for instance, has developed a sensitive terminal bud. As a result, the cabbage relatives all seem a bit touchy and, under certain conditions, will deteriorate rapidly. All seem to benefit from association with aromatic herbs.

Carrots. Carrots produce a root exudate that has a beneficial effect on peas. Carrots also grow well with Brussels sprouts, cabbage, leaf lettuce, red radishes, and chives. In short, the carrot is an all-around plant in companionability.

Cauliflower. Cauliflower is another member of the cabbage family, with most of the family's usual wants and needs. It is greatly influenced by aromatic herbs.

Corn. Corn has interesting relationships with a lot of plants. It is stimulated by both peas and beans—probably because these two add nitrogen to the soil in usable form. Corn also has a beneficial effect on cucumbers, melons, squash, and other vine crops.

Cucumbers. Cucumbers are very adaptable in the garden. The plants grow well intermixed with corn or cabbage, and they like nearby companion plantings of such paired vegetables as lettuce and bush beans or lettuce and radishes.

Kale. Kale does well planted with its relative cabbage. It is also benefitted by being planted near aromatic herbs.

Lettuce. Lettuce seems to be a very chummy vegetable. It grows well in combination with beets and cabbage—that is, all three together. It aids onions and is itself aided by the presence of carrots.

Melons. Cantaloupes like to be near corn.

Onions. Onions and cabbage do well together. Onions like to grow with beets and seem to be benefitted by lettuce and summer savory, but apparently inhibit the growth of beans and peas.

Peas. Peas are one of those great plants that seem to help almost everything. In particular, they fix nitrogen in the soil so that other plants can use it. They especially like beans, carrots, cucumbers, corn, radishes, and turnips. They are retarded, however, by onions and garlic.

Peppers. Peppers are relatives of tomatoes and eggplant and can be grown among them without problem. Onions and carrots do well sown among pepper plants.

Radishes. Radishes and peas are mutually beneficial, and pole beans are aided by radishes. Nasturtiums give radishes a great flavor, and leaf lettuce makes them tender.

Spinach. Spinach helps to maintain soil microorganisms and soil moisture. It also produces an exudate that stimulates other vegetables like cabbage.

Squash. Like other vines, squash likes to grow among corn plants.

Tomatoes. Tomatoes and asparagus are mutually beneficial, and parsley helps both. Tomatoes also do well grown near cabbage and mustard greens. Outside of that, they seem to prefer to be left alone and to grow year after year in the same spot.

Turnips and Rutabagas. Turnips and rutabagas are mutually helpful; and turnips are just generally helpful to a number of other vegetables.

Many herbs are quite pungent, and their scents can permeate the garden, especially if you occasionally crush a few of their leaves or stems to release the oils. Many old-time gardeners swear that herbs are cure-alls for everything that ails the garden—from bad vibes to crows to insects. If nothing else, with herbs you'll have the smelliest garden in town.

Companion Herbs

Basil. Sweet basil is generally beneficial to vegetables and is often planted near lettuce.

Chives. Like most other herbs, chives seem generally good for the garden. They especially stimulate the growth of carrots and tomatoes.

Dill. Dill in small quantities has a beneficial effect. It is especially good with cabbages. Mature dill, however, retards carrots and tomatoes.

Garlic. As a member of the onion family, garlic has the same effects as onions. (See above.)

Marjoram. Some people insist that sweet marjoram is absolutely indispensable in the vegetable garden and stimulates almost everything.

Mint. Mint is generally beneficial to the garden and seems to repel many kinds of insects and pests.

Oregano. As a close relative of sweet marjoram, oregano is considered equally helpful in the garden generally.

Parsley. Parsley stimulates tomatoes and corn, especially when grown between the plants.

Rosemary. Rosemary and sage stimulate one another, and rosemary generally is beneficial to the garden.

Sage. Sage is especially helpful to cabbage, protecting it from some pests and making it more tender. Generally sage is helpful to all plants.

Savory. Summer savory is beneficial to onions and to beans.

Tarragon. Some gardeners favor tarragon as much as they do sweet marjoram, in insisting that it be planted in every vegetable garden.

Thyme. Thyme seems generally beneficial.

Herbs also repel a number of insects. This we will take up in the next chapter.

Making Companion Planting Work

Again I must tell you that, although plants do have an effect on other plants and all living things, our knowledge in this area is extremely limited and often tentative. Nevertheless I have had a lot of fun experimenting in my own garden, and I'm sure you can too. Not everything that I've mentioned will necessarily work for you, but some things will. After all, vegetable gardening should be considered one of those fun hobbies that offer something unexpected around every cabbage or stalk. In the garden diagrams in Chapter 2 I gave you some ideas on how to use companion plantings of vegetables and herbs for maximum effect. But that's just a start, and it's up to you to try out some of the additional information presented in this chapter.

If you'd like to explore this area further, you'll find the book *Companion Plants and How to Use Them* by Helen Philbrick and Richard Gregg (Old Greenwich, Conn.: Devin-Adair Company, 1966) a world of useful information.

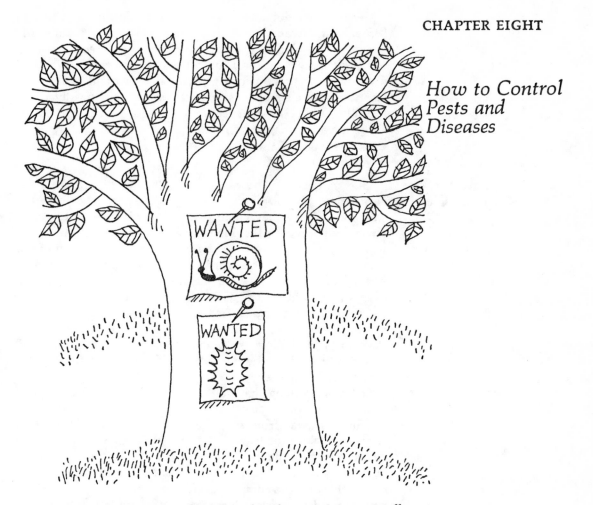

CHAPTER EIGHT

How to Control Pests and Diseases

What is it about bugs in the garden that causes a normally sane gardener to rush indoors, grab a spray can, and pour clouds of chemical spray all over a garden? This seems to be a form of insect-insanity. Now, warfare may be justified if the garden is being overrun by hoards of insects, but I've seen gardeners do this when I couldn't find more than two bedraggled bugs in the whole garden.

That kind of vigilance is absolutely unnecessary. There are many factors determining whether or not a particular insect attacks your garden. Weather has a lot to do with it. Insects move from one place to another and are often influenced by temperatures and day lengths (which also affect vegetables, of course); any change can send them out of your garden and off in another direction.

Generally we don't use chemical insecticides or fungicides in IPS gardens because they destroy the balance of nature. For one thing, they kill or scare off organisms and insects that help our garden as well as those that we want to get rid of. What we want to do is to keep our gardens vigorous and healthy by resorting to the simplest, safest, easiest methods possible. The IPS rule is this: Use whatever works and don't hassle too much. There are a lot of ways to do that.

Being Mr. or Mrs. Clean

One gardener I know kept complaining bitterly that his garden was always overrun with insect pests, and indeed it was. Sometimes they almost wiped everything out. I had always felt sorry for the poor guy as he poured out his tale of woe, until one day I stopped by to see what the problem was. The minute I saw his garden I knew exactly what had happened. The place was a mess: there were piles of brush everywhere, scattered scraps of lumber around the edges, and leaves and other organic material within a few feet of his growing vegetables.

What he'd done was to create great hiding places and breeding grounds for both insects and diseases. His poor garden didn't have a chance.

So the first thing that you do is to keep your garden area clean. Get rid of all dead weeds; clean up piles of trash; move any lumber away from the edge of your garden; and don't let fruit, vegetables, or leaves lie on the surface. Simply haul the refuse away. Some organic materials can be put into your compost pile. (However, if you have diseased plants, don't throw them on the compost heap; burn them.)

These rules of cleanliness are extremely elementary, yet vitally important if you intend to garden without resorting to a full-scale chemical attack.

Getting Physical with Those Insects

All you really have to do with some insects is simply pluck them off with your fingers or spray them off with a water hose. These methods work well with slow-moving creatures. Insects with wings, of course, may often just fly away and laugh at you from another plant—but not always, though. Thus it's worth trying to eradicate them by knocking or hosing them. If insects do reappear in your garden, in the same or even greater numbers after you've tried simple methods, then you can haul out some bigger guns.

So you've tried cleanliness and physical therapy, and they don't work well enough. Well, don't give up yet. The next thing to try is soap and water. Although you can hardly use a chisel to pry scale insects like aphids off your plants, often soap and water will do the trick. Simply mix about 20 tablespoons of soap flakes (such as Ivory) in 6 gallons of water. Then put the mixture in a spray can or tank and go after your plants. (The diluted soap won't hurt your plants.) You'll be surprised how good this is.

The Soap and Water Treatment

I always feel that I've had the last laugh when I turn friendly insects loose in the garden and they go around gobbling up the pests that have been destroying my beloved vegetables. There are some great predator insects just ready and waiting to go to work for you: lacewing flies (the larvae really go after aphids), ladybugs (they have a greedy appetite for aphids, thrips, tree lice, and the eggs and larvae of many other plant-destroying insects), praying mantises (the young eat aphids, flies, and other small insects; and larger adults consume massive quantities of beetles, caterpillars, grasshoppers, and other damaging garden pests), and trichogramma wasps (they're especially effective on the larvae of the cabbage worm). In the appendix you'll find the names and adddresses of companies that sell predator insects.

Mother Nature's Insect Predators

GOOD BUGS

Mechanical Bugaboos

Some pests can be killed off or repelled easily, using simple devices placed about in your garden. Slugs and snails seem such a problem, for instance, that some gardeners give up and don't bother to do anything to get rid of them. The salvation is so simple that you'll hardly believe it. In researching the slug problem, a prominent scientific institution tried a number of very elaborate methods to eradicate snails and slugs and finally after many years of experimentation stumbled on an answer: Just put out shallow saucers of beer around the garden at night. Slugs and snails are attracted by this beer and drown in the liquid.

Maybe you're having trouble with earwigs (they're the menacing-looking bugs with the big pincers; you'll never forget them once you've seen one). Try rolling up a newspaper and putting it near the problem plants. Earwigs will hide inside the rolled-up newspaper in droves. Then you can simply burn them up.

Companion Plants

Here's our old friend from the last chapter: plants that affect other plants or animals. Some gardeners are enthusiastic about this method of using special plants or herbs to repel insects; other gardenrs aren't so sure. The truth is that, although scientific research has proven that some plants do repel pests (marigolds, for instance, repel or kill nematodes, a variety of parasitic worms that live in the soil), it has not verified the claims made for many plants. Therefore, you will have to experiment yourself and see what works in your own garden. Here are some theories:

Chives, a member of the onion family, are said to repel many kinds of insects.

Garlic, also a member of the onion family, is often attributed with great powers. It is said to control blight and to repel or kill aphids, mosquito larvae, some types of caterpillars, and sucking bugs.

Leek, another member of the onion family, is said to help repel the carrot fly.

Marigolds excrete a substance from their roots that kills nematodes in the soil. This phenomenon seems well proven. Some gardeners also believe that marigolds kill the whitefly on tomatoes.

Mint is said to repel ants and cabbage-worm butterflies.

Nasturtiums are said to repel squash bugs.

Radishes are said to repel the striped cucumber beetle.

Rosemary is said to repel the carrot fly.

Sage is thought to protect plants against the cabbage butterfly.

Tomatoes planted near cabbage are believed to help repel the white cabbage butterfly.

Plant Sprays

Many gardeners believe not only that living plants repel insects but also that their leaves or petals can be liquified and turned into effective sprays that give your gardens strong protection.

Here are a couple of methods you can try. For either method you simply pick the plants with the most disagreeable odors, such as garlic, marigolds, and chives (just one garlic clove is enough, however).

In the first method, you put your clove, petals, and leaves in a pot or pan, add enough water to cover the ingredients, bring the mixture to the boiling point, and then turn off the heat. Strain off the solid particles, dilute the remaining liquid with 4 to 5 parts of water, and stir for 5 to 10 minutes. Now you're ready to spray.

In the second method, drop the clove, petals, and leaves into a blender. Put in enough water to cover and turn on the blender. Blend until the contents seem fairly liquified. Strain off the solid particles (if any), add about 2 to 3 teaspoons of the remaining liquid to 1 quart of water, and use the diluted mixture in your sprayer.

The leaves of such companion plants as mint, rosemary, and radishes can similarly be turned into sprays, to be used against the specific pests that they're supposed to repel.

Biological Sprays

Today there are spray preparations on the market that contain bacterial organisms that kill some kinds of insects. One of them, Thuricide (containing *Bacillus thuringiensis*) paralyzes the digestive system of such leaf-chewing worms as caterpillars, cabbage loopers, and tomato hornworms without having any deleterious effect on birds, bees, pets, or humans. You will find this preparation available at many nurseries and listed in many of the seed catalogs of companies cited in the appendix.

Botanical Sprays

There are also extremely effective botanical sprays that you can buy: pyrethrum (which is made from certain chrysanthemum flowers), rotenone (which is derived from the roots of certain tropical plants), and ryania (which is made from the stems of a tropical shrub). Ask your nurseryman for these.

In the chart accompanying this chapter there are suggestions on which sprays will work best for you in attacking the pests in your garden.

Plant Diseases   Generally IPS gardeners are organic gardeners and don't use chemical preparations to fight plant diseases, blight, and fungi. In an IPS garden we keep disease to a minimum without chemical help by resorting chiefly to two procedures: planting disease-resistant varieties of seeds and seedlings and destroying diseased plants whenever we find them in our garden.

Rooting out and burning diseased vegetation is part of the cleanliness that I mentioned earlier. A few of the most common diseases that you may encounter are mildew (appearing as a white or gray, powdery or downy coating on leaves and stems), rust (appearing first as whitish pustules or warts on the underside of leaves, then as powdery red or brown spores carried by the wind), blight and scab (both appearing as spreading yellow, brown, or red spots on leaves, especially shaded lower leaves), and wilt and root rot (both causing decayed roots and revealed by the wilting of foliage).

As for planting disease-resistant seeds and seedlings, we can note that currently there is much research under way to produce vegetable varieties that are resistant to major plant diseases. Each year something new reaches the market. Currently, for instance, there are cabbage strains resistant to virus yellows; cucumber strains resistant to anthracnose, downy mildew, mosaic, powdery mildew, and scab; cantaloupes resistant to fusarium and powdery mildew; and snapbeans resistant to mosaic, powdery mildew, and root rot. You can get these and other disease-resistant varieties from seed catalogs or seed racks; the catalog descriptions or package labels will state the diseases to which the varieties are resistant.

Although I don't recommend chemical preparations (such as captan and phaltan) to combat plant diseases, I will say that they can be quite effective. I should also note that most seeds purchased from seed companies have already been treated with fungicides. You can buy untreated seeds from some companies, but you must usually specify untreated seeds in your order.

Organic gardeners, as I've already emphasized, don't like chemical sprays because they consider them destructive to the cycles of nature. Organic gardeners simply learn to live with some insects because they recognize that none of the organic control methods is 100 percent effective.

There is no doubt that chemical pesticides do a far superior job of killing insects. For this reason I want to mention three: diazinion, malathion, and sevin. Diazinion is especially good for controlling root maggots. And between this chemical and the other two it's possible to handle effectively almost any insect that invades your garden. One of the many problems, of course, is that these insecticides kill the "good" insects like ladybugs and mantises as well as the insects that you want to get rid of.

Whether or not you use chemical sprays will depend on you. I never use anything like them in my garden, and I have very little trouble.

So that gives you a rundown on what you can do to control insect pests and diseases without making your garden an armed camp. In most cases an IPS garden won't really have these problems very seriously anyway because your vegetables will be healthy, fast-growing, and moderately disease-resistant. If and when you do have trouble, however, it's best to try the easiest way first, moving on to the really big artillery like spray guns only when they're really needed.

In addition to insects and diseases, some species of animals are found to be a nuisance in the garden.

Gophers can be driven out of your garden by using a device marketed under the name Klipty-Klop (available at many garden centers). It is essentially a small windmill that sets up a vibration in the ground that gophers can't tolerate.

Rabbits can be held off by completely surrounding your small plot with a chicken wire fence.

Birds are a mixed blessing. They do feed on damaging insects, and thus many gardeners build birdhouses to attract birds into their gardens. On the other hand, some birds will eat tiny seedlings or such fruit as tomatoes, and thus you may have to drive them off if they get too pesky. One defense is to hang metal foil strips on strings extended two or three feet over your garden. An extreme measure would be to enclose your garden completely—sides and top—with gauze or chicken wire held up by posts or a frame.

Chemical Sprays

Animal Protection

What Kind of Control Do You Use For What Pest?

Vegetable	Symptoms	Pests
Asparagus	Shoots channeled, leaves eaten by larvae or beetles	Asparagus beetle
Beans	Colonies of black sucking insects on leaves	Aphids
	Circular holes eaten in leaves	Bean leaf beetles
	Small plants cut off at soil level at night	Cutworm
	Hopping, running insects that suck sap from leaves	Leafhoppers
	Lower surface of leaves eaten between veins; skeletonized	Mexican bean beetles
	Scaly nymphs on underside of leaves; white adults flutter about when disturbed	Whiteflies
Beets	Leaves eaten, leaving trail of silver slime	Snails and slugs
Broccoli	Colonies of small green insects on leaves	Aphids
	Plants sickly; maggots attack underground parts of plant	Cabbage maggots
	Holes in leaves eaten by larvae	Cabbage worms and loopers
	Small plants cut off at soil level at night	Cutworms
Brussels Sprouts	Colonies of small insects on leaves	Aphids
	Plants sickly; maggots attack underground parts of plant	Cabbage maggots
	Holes eaten in leaves by larvae	Cabbage worms and loopers
	Small plants cut off at soil level at night	Cutworms
Cabbage	Colonies of small insects on leaves	Aphids
	Plants sickly; maggots attack underground parts of plant	Cabbage maggots
	Holes eaten in leaves by larvae	Cabbage worms and loopers
	Small plants cut off at soil level at night	Cutworms
Cauliflower	Colonies of small green insects on leaves	Aphids

Remedy

Pick off	Hose off with water	Spray with soap solution	Spray with Thuricide	Spray with pyrethrum	Spray with rotenone	Spray with ryania	Put paper collar around lower stem of plant, extending into soil.	Put wood ash around base of plant.	Put out containers of beer.	Trap in rolled-up newspapers.	Locate grub by "sawdust frass" around bored hole in stem; slit stem carefully with sharp knife and remove grub; mound earth over slit and along stem.
X				X	X	X					
	X	X		X	X	X					
X				X	X	X					
							X				
X				X	X	X					
				X	X	X					
				X	X						
									X		
	X	X		X	X	X					
								X			
X			X	X							
							X				
	X	X		X	X	X					
								X			
X			X	X							
							X				
	X	X		X	X	X					
								X			
X			X	X							
							X				
	X	X		X	X	X					

117

What Kind of Control Do You Use For What Pest?

Vegetable	Symptoms	Pests
Cauliflower, continued	Plants sickly; maggots attack stems and underground parts of plant	Cabbage maggots
	Holes in leaves eaten by larvae	Cabbage worms and loopers
Corn	Silks cut off at ear; kernels destroyed by fairly large larvae	Corn earworms
	Ears and stalks tunneled by larvae	Corn borers
	Small plants cut off at soil level at night	Cutworms
Cucumber	Colonies of small insects on underside of leaves	Aphids
	All parts eaten	Cucumber beetles
	All parts of vines eaten	Pickleworm
Eggplant	Plants defoliated (beetles are black striped, larvae brick red)	Colorado potato beetles
	Colonies of small insects on underside of leaves	Aphids
	Colonies on underside of leaves	Eggplant lacebugs
Lettuce	Colonies of small insects on leaves	Aphids
	Leaves eaten by pincer bugs	Earwigs
	Wedge-shaped insects found on leaves; tips of leaves turn brown	Leafhoppers
	Leaves eaten, leaving trails of silver slime	Snails and slugs
Kale	Colonies of small insects on leaves	Aphids
	Small pin-size holes chewed in leaves	Flea beetles
Melons	Colonies of small insects on underside of leaves	Aphids
	All parts of plant eaten	Cucumber beetles
Mustard Greens	Colonies of small insects on leaves	Aphids
	Leaves with holes eaten by larvae	Cabbage worms
	Plants sickly; maggots attack root and stem underground	Root maggots
Onions	Older leaves wither; small yellow insects feed at base of leaves	Onion thrips
	Plants sickly; maggots attack parts below ground	Onion maggots

Remedy

Pick off	Hose off with water	Spray with soap solution	Spray with Thuricide	Spray with pyrethrum	Spray with rotenone	Spray with ryania	Put paper collar around lower stem of plant, extending into soil.	Put wood ash around base of plant.	Put out containers of beer.	Trap in rolled-up newspapers.	Locate grub by "sawdust frass" around bored hole in stem; slit stem carefully with sharp knife and remove grub; mound earth over slit and along stem.
								X			
X			X		X						
X						X					
X											
							X				
	X	X		X	X	X					
X				X	X	X					
X				X	X	,					
X				X	X	X					
	X	X		X	X	X					
						X					
	X	X		X	X	X					
				X	X	X				X	
									X		
	X	X		X	X	X					
X				X	X	X					
	X	X		X	X	X					
X				X	X	X					
	X	X		X	X	X					
X			X		X						
								X			
				X	X	X					
								X			

What Kind of Control Do You Use For What Pest?

Vegetable	Symptoms	Pests
Okra	Holes eaten in pods	Corn earworms
Peas	Terminals deformed; colonies of small insects on leaves	Pea aphids
	Beetles feed on blooms; larvae bore through pod and enter young peas	Pea weevils
Peppers	Colonies of small insects on leaves	Aphids
	Plants defoliated by orange and yellow bodied beetles	Blister beetles
	Small plants cut off at soil level at night	Cutworms
	Small pin-size holes chewed in leaves	Flea beetles
	Leaves and fruit eaten	Pepper weevils
Radishes	Plants sickly; maggots attack plants below ground	Root maggots
Spinach	Colonies of small insects on leaves	Aphids
	Larvae tunnel through leaves	Spinach leaf miners
Squash	Colonies of small insects underneath the leaves	Aphids
	All parts eaten	Cucumber beetles
	Plants wilted (brownish flat bug)	Squash bug
	Sudden wilting of runners; holes in stem near base	Squash vine borer
Swiss Chard	Colonies of small insects on leaves	Aphids
Tomatoes	Colonies of small insects on leaves	Aphids
	Small plants cut off at soil level	Cutworms
	Many shot-size holes in leaves	Flea beetles
	Leaves eaten (large green worm with horn)	Tomato hornworm
	Scale-like nymphs attached to underside of leaves	Whiteflies

Remedy

Pick off	Hose off with water	Spray with soap solution	Spray with Thuricide	Spray with pyrethrum	Spray with rotenone	Spray with ryania	Put paper collar around lower stem of plant, extending into soil.	Put wood ash around base of plant.	Put out containers of beer.	Trap in rolled-up newspapers.	Locate grub by "sawdust frass" around bored hole in stem; slit stem carefully with sharp knife and remove grub; mound earth over stem and along stem.
X						X					
	X	X		X	X	X					
X											
	X	X		X	X	X					
X				X	X	X					
							X				
				X	X	X					
X											
								X			
	X	X		X	X	X					
					X						
	X	X		X	X	X					
X				X	X	X					
X				X	X	X					
											X
	X	X		X	X	X					
	X	X		X	X	X					
							X				
				X	X	X					
X			X	X	X	X					
				X	X						

CHAPTER NINE

How to Water
the Garden

Watering your Intensive Postage Stamp garden, like doing everything else recommended in this book, should be simple and easy. It *is* simple and easy, but it is also absolutely crucial to the success of your garden. The truth is that water—or the lack of it—can sometimes create tremendous garden problems. A gardening friend of mine, for instance spent hours on end spading his plot and staking out the sections and planting the various vegetables. When thereafter it came time to water, however, he couldn't seem to find the time. As a result, some of his cabbages cracked, and his other vegetables just didn't turn out right. He of course blamed his failure on bad luck, but actually his entire problem was poor watering.

Without enough water, bean pods produce only a few seeds and the rest of the pods shrivel, beets become stringy, radishes get pithy, cucumbers stop growing well, and more. Once started, vegetables must grow rapidly without interruptions or slowdowns. Stop growth by checking the water supply, and you really set your vegetables back. Agronomists tell us that when a plant isn't getting enough water it's under "water stress." And although this may be useful for flowers, since water stress can induce blooming,· it nearly always sets vegetables back. Once set back they never seem to recover.

You've heard that old saying, "Damned if you do, and damned if you don't." Well, watering is like that in a vegetable garden. It's absolutely essential, but it can also create problems. Water itself is a nutrient used directly by the plants, and it also dissolves and carries other nutrients to the roots. *That's the good part.* The roots of plants also need air just like we do. Oxygen must reach the roots, and carbon dioxide must be given off by the roots to return to the air. Most soil has enough air space for this exchange to take place. If you eliminate the oxygen by filling all the soil space continually with water, however, root growth stops; and if this condition continues long enough, the plant dies. *That's the bad part.*

An ideal soil for plant growth contains 50 percent solid matter, 50 percent pore space (that's what our IPS soil has). About half this pore space should be occupied by water, and that's the object of your watering program.

The general rule for watering IPS gardens is this: Water thoroughly, regularly, and infrequently. When you soak the soil thoroughly, you add water until it reaches "field capacity" —that is, roughly all the water that the air spaces of the soil can hold. And you want to keep your garden between this condition and the point at which moisture is so scarce that plant roots can no longer take water from the soil.

Whenever you water your IPS beds you want to water them thoroughly to a depth of about 3 feet. The length of time that it takes to water this deep will depend on the type of soil under the bed, but it will usually take at least an hour or two. A good rule is to simply water until you can easily sink a stick about 3 feet deep. If there are a lot of rocks below your IPS subsoil, you may not be able to do this; then just estimate. After thoroughly watering your beds, don't water again until the soil has almost dried out to a depth of 10 inches. Just take a trowel and check. If the soil is almost dry to this depth, water deeply again—and then don't water until the moisture has receded to 10 inches again.

At some times of the year, as when it's cool or rainy, this interval between waterings may extend two weeks or more; but when it's hot and dry you may have to water every five or six days. Thus it generally doesn't matter one bit whether or not it rains. You simply don't water until your 10-inch trowel test shows that watering is necessary. By letting the soil almost dry out this way, you give it a chance to take in a good supply of air as the water supply is removed.

After a few years of vegetable gardening, you'll have acquired enough experience to sense whenever watering is necessary and how much to water. You'll have adjusted to the special needs of your climate and seasonal rainfall.

Which Way to Water

Some gardeners insist that the only way to water an IPS garden is with a hose lying on the ground. Others simply set up a sprinkler in the middle of their bed and turn it on when it's time to water.

What should you do?

I personally feel that you should do whatever is easiest (using either a hose or a sprinkler), so long as you water thoroughly until the soil reaches field capacity. Then don't water again until the soil is almost dried out.

In my own case, I usually set up a sprinkler in the garden and turn it on a regular intervals. This is easy and simple. There's no doubt that cool-season root crops take well to this method. But overhead watering like this can damage hot-weather crops like squash and tomatoes (tomatoes will crack). You can prevent tomato cracking and other problems by watering overhead until the plants start to produce fruit and then use a ground hose after that.

As a rule, you should water in the morning during the spring and fall (that is, in cool weather) and in the evening during the summer heat. (If you live in an area where the humidity is high—like along the coast or in a region with lots of fog—

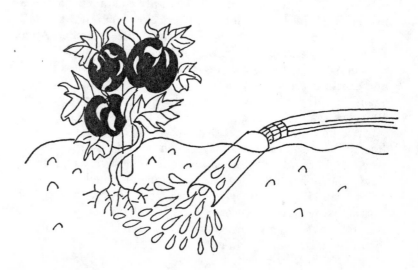

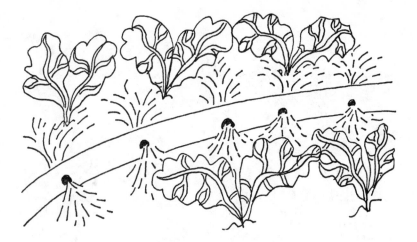

overhead sprinkling can encourage mildew. You can generally overcome this by watering in the morning so that the plants are dry by evening.)

If you find that the leaves of your vegetables wilt somewhat during the hot summer, don't panic. Actually some plants deliberately let their leaves droop in order to prevent the hot sun from drawing moisture from their exposed flat surfaces. A squash vine, for instance, that looks quite wilted in the afternoon will snap back next morning crisp and fresh.

Besides watering the garden with a hose or a sprinkler, some gardeners really Rube Goldberg it and wind up with all sorts of innovations. For deep-rooted plants like tomatoes, for instance, you can push a piece of 2-inch hollow pipe six to twelve inches into the soil and then send water down the pipe to those deep roots. Or you can lay out two or three pieces of perforated plastic pipe or hose just under the vegetable leaves in your garden. When you're ready to water just attach a hose and allow the water to trickle out.

In sum, that's the watering system for our IPS beds. Water deeply, and then don't water again until the soil is almost dry.

Do this and not only will your garden work its heart out growing big healthy, tender vegetables for your dinner table, but sometimes it'll produce so much extra that you'll wind up having to beg the neighbors to take the surplus off your hands. When this happens, you can pat yourself on the back. Not only have you mastered the techniques of growing lots of vegetables in a very small space but you're well on your way to becoming a wise and enlightened harvester of the fruits of nature.

Now Break Out the Seed Catalogs

Okay, so now you know how to grow Intensive Postage Stamp gardens and produce all you can eat in a very small space. I do hope that, as you garden from here on out, you'll try as many of the suggested garden combinations as possible.

Maybe, for instance, you might try one of the standard vegetable gardens the first year, all compact and by itself; then the next year you might grow corn in 4-by-4-foot boxes, root crops in a special garden, and other vegetables in other special gardens.

Or maybe you'd like to try several kinds of gardens all at once—flower bed gardens with vegetables, boxes, and ground gardens in various shapes, while at the same time trying to coax out more and more vegetables. That's really part of the fun and excitement of IPS gardening—its continual opportunities for experimentation.

The best thing about IPS gardening, of course, is that it's simple, easy, and in balance with nature, making the soil better and more productive each and every season.

And if in the beginning you started out with a brown thumb like I did, somewhere along the way you're bound to discover that it isn't brown at all any more but has turned to a very satisfying green.

APPENDICES AND GLOSSARY

APPENDIX A
How to Compost

APPENDIX B
Suppliers That Distribute Seed Catalogs

Glossary

Index

How to Compost

For the amateur gardener the word *composting* is often terrifying. It should not be. A compost pile is simply any collected mixture of vegetation, manure, or other organic materials that is allowed to decay and is then used for fertilizing and soil conditioning. It can be simply an unconfined heap or it can be enclosed in a bin or other container. It usually takes a while to make one because it takes a while to collect the material and another while for the material to "ripen," but anyone can compost successfully.

Before learning some specific methods of building compost, you should be aware of certain principles governing "traditional" composting. You should know that good old-fashioned composting depends primarily on particle size, on the amount of nitrogen available, on the heat produced, on the moisture of the pile, and on whether or not the pile is turned over periodically.

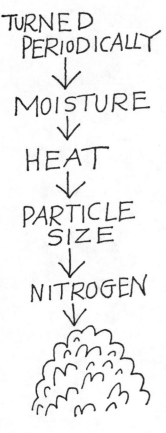

TURNED
PERIODICALLY
↓
MOISTURE
↓
HEAT
↓
PARTICLE
SIZE
↓
NITROGEN
↓

1. The smaller the particle size, generally the faster the decomposition, because bacteria can then attack more surface area faster. Thus, if the leaves, stems, and other materials are shredded into small pieces before being added to the compost pile, they'll decay quicker and be ready sooner.

2. The bacteria in the pile need nitrogen. If there is too much organic material (carbon) in proportion to the available nitrogen, the bacteria will not work as fast, and the decomposition will go slowly. The evidence of this will be poor heat production in the compost pile. Generally you can correct this deficiency by adding nitrogen in the form of fresh manure or blood meal here and there throughout the pile.

3. A compost pile must heat up for good bacterial action to occur. The degree of heat depends on the size of the pile. If the pile isn't high enough, it will lose heat, and bacterial action will slow down. Too high a pile is also bad, because it will then be compressed too much, shutting off the air supply to the bacteria.

4. Every pile also needs moisture for decomposition to take place. A moisture content of about 40 to 60 percent is about right; more than this can cut down on the oxygen available to the bacteria. You can keep your pile at about the right moisture content by making sure that it remains about as wet as a squeezed-out wet sponge. Just put your hand in the pile and feel. (Watch out, however, for it can be really hot—about 130° to 160° F.) If it doesn't seem moist enough, just add water with a hose until it has the right consistency.

5. A compost pile also needs turning. Using a manure fork or a shovel, turn it so that the top and side materials become the center. This allows air penetration and also brings raw matter to the center where more action is taking place.

When finished or "ripe," the materials placed in the compost pile will have been converted into a crumbly brown substance with the fragrance of good earth. It's then ready to use. (The volume of organic materials, by the way, will have decreased considerably. As decomposition proceeds, most piles shrink to about half their original size; a 5-foot pile, for instance, will end up hardly more than 2½ feet high. One cubic foot of ripe compost is usually enough to make up 4 square feet of an IPS garden.)

I'm now going to show you how to make compost piles with almost no effort. I'll also show you some more complicated ways to make compost. Remember, though, we're dedicated to doing things easy. After all, mother nature doesn't care. Just provide her with the right conditions (no matter how quickly or easily you created them), and she'll work hard for you.

You can produce an entirely acceptable compost in a garbage can, placed either outdoors or in a corner of your garage. The method isn't governed by all the principles outlined above, and it doesn't have all the refinements of some of those bulky piles out in the garden, but it works, and that's what counts. Now here's how you do it.

1. Buy a galvanized garbage can (a 20- or 30-gallon size), and in it put a garbage can liner (the plastic kind).

2. Inside on the bottom of the liner put a 2-inch layer of soil or peat moss.

3. Add randomly almost any kind of waste kitchen materials —scraps from the table, vegetable and fruit leftovers, orange peels, coffee grounds, tea leaves, egg shells, and so on. Although you can also add garden wastes such as grass clippings and leaves, you want to use mostly garbage, because you want a moist, gooey, rotting mixture for quick results.

4. Always keep the lid on the garbage can between additions of new material. You want to keep air out.

5. When the can is full, put it out in the hot sun and let it stand covered and untouched for about 3 weeks. The heat will cook it, and it will then be ready for use.

Some people object to this method, complaining that the compost smells excessively. It does. Unlike most other kinds of composting, this one uses anaerobic bacteria (the kind that don't need air). You don't have to expose the odor, however. Just close off the plastic liner with a wire twist, and keep the lid on the can.

Household Garbage

Soil

Using a Plastic Bag

This method is essentially identical to the one just given, except that no garbage can is used.

1. Buy a dark-colored plastic bag, the kind used to line 20- or 30-gallon garbage cans.

2. Inside, put a 2-inch layer of soil or peat moss.

3. Add randomly any kind of waste kitchen materials (as noted before) and maybe occasionally garden wastes.

4. When full, set the bag out in full sunlight for about 3 weeks. The compost will then be ready to use.

Using Another Garbage Can

Here is a longer but more customary method of composting. Using a garbage can, though, makes it somewhat unusual.

1. Buy a galvanized garbage can (a 20- or 30-gallon size), and punch several small holes in the bottom. Put the can up on a few bricks, and place a pan underneath to catch any liquid that might drain out from the moisture contained in the decaying garbage that you will be adding.

2. Inside on the bottom of the can put a 3-inch layer of soil or peat moss.

3. If you like, buy some red worms—the fishing kind—and add them to the soil at the bottom.

4. Add 2 to 3 inches of kitchen garbage, then a 2-inch layer of grass clippings and leaves, another layer of kitchen garbage, a layer of grass clippings and leaves, and so on until the can is full.

5. Put the lid on the can. The ripe compost will be ready in about 3 or 4 months. If you start the can in the fall, the compost will be ready to add to your garden by spring. (You don't need to worry about the moisture content of this kind of pile, nor does it need to be turned.)

132

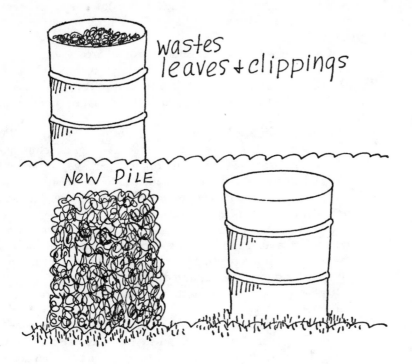

wastes
leaves + clippings

NEW PILE

If you have a space problem in your yard or if you simply want to confine your compost pile to a small space, here's a good method.

1. Buy or find a large barrel—the 50- to 55-gallon kind. It can be wooden, or it can be one of those big steel oil drums. Cut the bottom and the top out, and set the barrel anywhere you wish on exposed soil. Make sure that you fashion some kind of tight-fitting lid for the top.

2. Put in a 6-inch layer of kitchen wastes, then a 2-inch layer of garden soil, and then a 2-inch layer of leaves, grass clippings, and other garden wastes. Repeat the layering as materials become available. You might also want to add red fishing worms to speed up the process.

3. When the barrel is full, lift it off the pile and start a new pile right next to it. The contents of the first pile will more or less stand alone without the support of the barrel.

4. Water and turn the compost as necessary. It will be ready for your garden in about 4 to 6 months.

Using a Barrel

Big Conventional Pile

Some gardeners aren't happy unless they're building a big messy compost pile out in the backyard. For these types, here's a method that will keep them happy for almost a quarter of the year.

1. Clear off a 5- or 6-foot-square ground area.

2. On top of the cleared area put down a 6-inch layer of fairly coarse material—twigs, brush, a few corn stalks, sunflower stalks, and so on. This provides ventilation underneath the pile.

3. Start building the main body of the heap in layers. Put down a 6-inch layer of vegetation materials—grass clippings, leaves, weeds, vegetable remains, organic garbage, and so on. On top of this greenery, add a 2-inch layer of fresh manure. (You can also add a thin layer of limestone to improve bacterial action and hasten the decomposition.)

4. For every two or three layers of vegetation (and manure), add a 1-inch layer of soil. This soil contains bacteria that will help break down the organic material. Now wet down the pile until it is just moist, not saturated.

5. Repeat this procedure until the pile reaches a height of about 5 feet.

6. When finished, add a thin covering of soil to the pile to help seal in the moisture. You must, however, also keep air flowing throughout the pile in order to keep the bacterial action high. Thus take a stick or thin pole and punch vertical holes into the top of the pile, reaching all the way to the bottom. Make the holes about 2 or 3 feet apart.

7. Always keep the moisture content of the pile at 40 to 60 percent—about the consistency, as I've said, of a squeezed-out wet sponge. Check the moisture by feeling inside the pile with your hand, and then add water whenever necessary. Watering may be required every 4 or 5 days in hot weather.

8. Except for watering, let the pile sit undisturbed for 2 to 3 weeks. Then turn it, putting the material from the top and sides into the middle. Turn it again at 3-week intervals. When the inside materials turn brownish and crumble on touch, you can be sure that the compost is ready for your garden.. This usually takes 3½ to 4 months.

The University of California Quick Method

In 1954 the University of California at its Organic Experimental Farm developed a composting method that's great for impatient types because the compost is ready in just 14 days. The decomposition is speeded up by shredding the materials

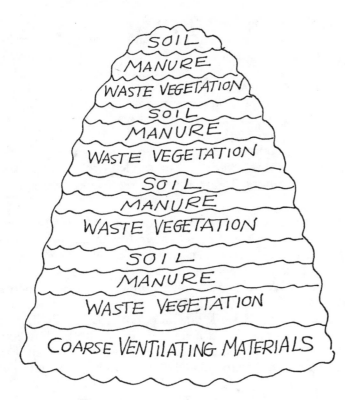

and mixing them all together so that the bacteria have many surfaces to work on at once.

1. Mix together one part fresh manure and two parts other compost ingredients (leaves, grass clippings, cut-up corn stalks, table scraps, and so on). You can obtain fresh manure from a local riding stable or from a nursery. It must be fresh, not processed, manure, however.

2. Using a rotary lawnmower, shred everything completely. (You have to catch everything in a bag, naturally.) Simply put down a small pile of materials and run the lawnmower over it. Then put down another pile and repeat the process. Better yet, use a power shredder; but, in any case, the materials must be shredded into very small particles for this method to work well.

3. Mix everything together, and form the mixture into a 4-foot high, 4-by-6-foot heap.

Now, here's what to expect.

4. By the second or third day the middle of the pile should have begun to heat up to about 130° to 160° F. If it hasn't, add more manure.

5. Turn the heap on the fourth day. Make sure that it's warm and moist. Simply put your hand inside, but be careful because it can be quite hot. If it doesn't feel moist to the touch, about like a squeezed-out wet sponge, add some water.

6. Turn the heap again on the seventh day.

7. Turn it once more on the tenth day. The heap should now have started to cool off, for it's almost ready.

8. It's ready on the fourteenth day. It won't look like fine humus, but the materials will have broken down into a dark, rich, fairly crumbly substance. You can let it rot further if you wish, or you can use it in your garden right away.

Composting in a Bin

Many gardeners like to put their compost in bins. There's no doubt that it's easier and neater to work with that way. After all, who likes a big, messy pile in the middle of the backyard— or even a little messy pile for that matter.

You can make a good compost bin with a few boards. Twelve pieces of board—each 12 inches wide, 1 inch thick, and 30 inches long—will work fine. Just take four of the boards and nail them together to make a frame or bottomless box. Using the remaining boards, make two more frames. You then set one frame on the ground and stack the other two on top of

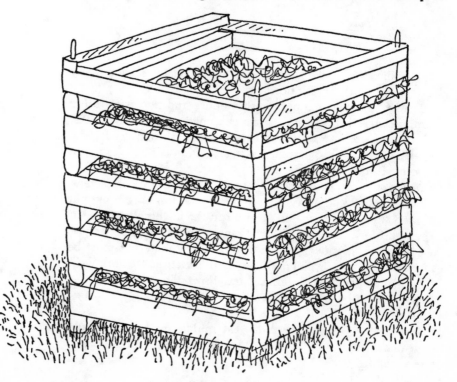

it to make a big bin. Now all you do is chop everything up with your lawnmower and throw it in. You then proceed, using whatever composting method suits you—either the "The Big, Conventional Pile" or "The University of California Quick Method."

You can steadily multiply these bins or piles easily by simply taking off the top frame after the compost has sunk below its level. Place it on the ground beside the other two and start to fill it with new materials for compost. As the compost in the first bin subsides some more, you take the second frame off and put it on your new bin. When finished, your original bottom frame goes on top of your new bin, forming a three-frame compost bin again.

A compost bin actually can be made from almost anything. Just make it about 3 feet high and about 2½ feet square. A neighbor of mine nailed four window screens together with a screen over the top to keep out flies. There are lots of other ways: concrete blocks, stones, a simple picket fence with slats, chicken wire, and more. Let your imagination soar, and see what you can come up with.

If you like, you can also buy a ready-made compost kit that includes a bin, instructions, and sometimes compost-maker tablets ("starters"). You can get one from many nurseries or by mail from many seed companies listed next in this appendix.

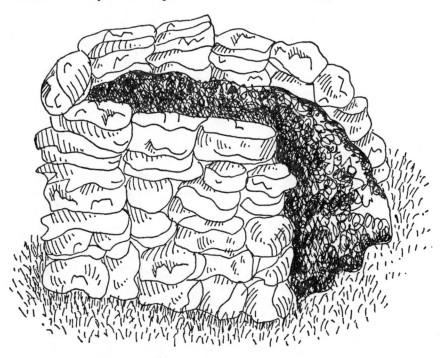

*Suppliers That
Distribute
Seed Catalogs*

Brecks of Boston, 200 Breck Building, Boston, Massachusetts 02110.

Burgess Seed and Plant Company, P.O. Box 3000, Galesburg, Michigan 49053. Their bright, attractive catalog contains special pages on gourmet vegetables and novelty varieties.

W. Atlee Burpee Company, P.O. Box 6929, Philadelphia, Pennsylvania 19132; Clinton, Iowa 52732; P.O. Box 748, 6350 Rutland Avenue, Riverside, California 92502. Burpee has three offices to serve eastern, mid-western, and far western customers respectively. A company prominent in horticultural and hybrid research, it grows most of the seeds that it sells. The very complete catalog illustrates garden supplies as well as vegetables and contains many helpful hints. The company also distributes a useful pamphlet, "Gardening for Pleasure: Helpful Hints for the Home Gardener."

D.V. Burrell Seed Growers Company, P.O. Box 150, Rocky Ford, Colorado 81067.

Comstock Ferre and Company, Wethersfield, Connecticut 06109.

De Giorgi Company, Inc., Council Bluffs, Iowa 51501. Their big catalog features prize-winning seeds.

Farmer Seed and Nursery Company, Faribault, Minnesota 55021. The company keeps in tune with latest developments in experimental agricultural stations. The catalog gives special attention to early-maturing vegetables.

Henry Field Seed and Nursery Company, 407 Sycamore Street, Shenandoah, Iowa 51602. The catalog contains a wide selection of vegetables, as well as many garden hints.

Gurney Seed and Nursery Company, 1448 Page Street, Yankton, South Dakota 57078. The catalog emphasizes varieties suited to northern climes.

Glecklers Seedmen, Metamora, Ohio 43540.

Joseph Harris Company, Inc., Moreton Farm, Rochester, New York 14624. Their extremely informative and well-designed catalog emphasizes varieties suitable for the northeastern states. They also issue a pamphlet, "Care of the Home Garden."

J.W. Jung Seed Company, Station 8, Randolph, Wisconsin 53956.

Kelly Brothers Nurseries, Inc., Dansville, New York 14437.

Earl May Seed and Nursery Company, 6032 Elm Street, Shenandoah, Iowa 51601.

McFayden, P.O. Box 1600, Brandon, Manitoba, Canada. The catalog contains a small, but unusual selection of vegetable varieties, especially suited for northern or Canadian climes.

J.E. Miller Nurseries, Inc., Canadaigua, New York 14424.

Nichols Garden Nursery, 1190 North Pacific Highway, Albany, Oregon 97321. They specialize in organic gardening, and their catalog features many unusual vegetable and herb seeds, including French, other European, and Oriental strains, as well as asparagus and rhubarb roots. The catalog even has a wine- and beer-making section.

L.L. Olds Seed Company, P.O. Box 1069, 2901 Packers Avenue, Madison, Wisconsin 53701.

George W. Park Seed Company, Inc., Greenwood, South Carolina 29646. This long-established Southern nursery offers a large selection of vegetable seeds.

Roswell Seed Company, P.O. Box 725, Roswell, New Mexico 88201. The catalog emphasizes seeds suited to the Southwest.

Seedway, Inc., Hall, New York 14463. The catalog contains planting instructions.

R.H. Shumway Seedsman, 628 Cedar Street, Rockford, Illinois 61101. The catalog is a kind of gem for its quaint, old-fashioned layout and illustrations; it offers many different vegetable varieties.

Stark Brothers Nurseries and Orchards, Louisiana, Missouri 63353.

Stokes Seeds, P.O. Box 548, Main Post Office, Buffalo, New York 14240. This is a northern company with many Canadian customers. The large catalog offers a huge selection of seeds, including seeds untreated with fungicide.

Otis S. Twilley Seed Company, Salisbury, Maryland 21801.

Suppliers that Distribute Catalogs of Herb Seeds and Plants

Burgess Seed and Plant Company (address above). Herbs are listed in the regular catalog.

W. Atlee Burpee Company (addresses above). The regular catalog illustrates a fair selection of herbs.

Capriland's Herb Farm, Silver Street, Coventry, Connecticut 06238.

Cedarbrook Herb Farm, Route 1, Box 1047, Sequim, Washington 93882. This small nursery mails herb plants in April, May, and June.

Comstock Ferre and Company, (address above). A separate herb catalog is available.

Farmer Seed and Nursery Company (address above). The regular catalog contains a small herb list, and the company also offers a free folder, "How to Grow a Kitchen Herb Garden."

Henry Field Seed and Nursery Company (address above).

Greene Herb Gardens, Greene, Rhode Island 02826.

Hemlock Hill Herb Farms, Litchfield, Connecticut 06759. The catalog offers perennial herb plants, including some old and rare varieties.

Le Jardin du Gourmet, Ramsey, New Jersey 07446. The chief emphasis is on herb plants and seeds, but also included are some imported vegetable seeds.

J.W. Jung Seed Company (address above). Herbs are listed in the regular catalog.

Merry Gardens, 1 Simonton Road, Camden, Maine 04842. The catalog costs 25 cents.

Mincemoyer's, Route 5, Box 379, Jackson, New Jersey 08527.

Nichols Garden Nursery (address above). The regular catalog contains an amazingly extensive selection of herb seeds.

L.L. Olds Seed Company (address above). Herbs are listed in the regular catalog.

R.H. Shumway Seedsman (address above). Herbs are listed in the regular catalog.

Otis S. Twilley Seed Company (address above). Herbs are listed in the regular catalog.

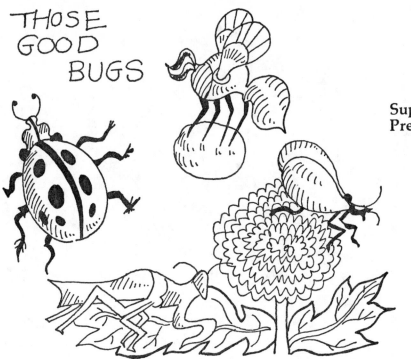

THOSE GOOD BUGS

**Suppliers of
Predator Insects**

Lacewing Flies
California Green Lacewings, Inc., 2521 Webb Avenue, Alameda, California 94501
Fairfax Biological Laboratory, Clinton Corners, New York 12514.
Gothard, Inc., P.O. Box 370, Canutillo, Texas 79835.

Ladybugs
Bio-Control Company, Route 2, Box 2397, Auburn, California 95603.
W. Atlee Burpee Company (addresses above).
Paul Harris, P.O. Box 1495, Marysville, California 95901.
L.E. Schnoor, P.O. Box 148, Yuba City, California 94991.

Praying Mantises
Bio-Control Company (address above).
W. Atlee Burpee Company (addresses above).
Eastern Biological Control Company, Route 5, Box 379, Jackson, New Jersey 08527.
Gothard, Inc. (address above).

Trichogramma Wasps
Fairfax Biological Laboratory (address above).
Gothard, Inc. (address above).

Cookbooks and Related Books for Home Gardeners

Dragonwagon, Crescent, *Putting Up Stuff for the Cold Time*, New York: Workman Publishing Co., 1972.

Farm Journal Food Editors, *America's Best Vegetable Recipes*, Garden City, N.Y.: Doubleday and Co, 1970.

Fox, Helen, *Gardening with Herbs for Flavor and Fragrance*, New York, Sterling Publishing Co, 1970.

Hertzberg, Ruth; Vaughn, Beatrice; and Greene, Janet, *Putting Food By*, Brattleboro, Vt.: Stephen Greene Press, 1973.

Hunter, Beatrice Trum, *Natural Foods Cookbook*, New York: Pyramid Publications.

Kraft, Ken, and Kraft, Pat, *Home Garden Cookbook*, Garden City, N.Y.: Doubelday and Co., 1970.

Rodale, Jerome I. *et al.*, *Country Gardener's Cookbook*, Emmaus, Pa.: Rodale Books.

———, *Stocking Up*, Emmaus, Pa.: Rodale Books, 1974.

Schuler, Stanley, *Gardens Are for Eating*, New York: Macmillan, 1971.

Schuler, Stanley, and Schuler, Elizabeth Meriweather, *Preserving the Fruits of the Earth*, New York: Dial Press, 1973.

U.S. Department of Agriculture, *Complete Guide to Home Canning*, New York: Dover Publications.

Wilder, Vicki, *In a Pickle or in a Jam*, Des Moines, Iowa: Better Homes and Gardens Press, 1971.

You can obtain much good gardening information from a wide variety of sources. The county agricultural agent in your area will often answer questions over the telephone and provide you with booklets on vegetable gardening, home canning, freezing, vegetable storage, and related subjects. His number should be listed in the telephone directory under county departments—usually under the title "Agriculture." The agent usually resides in the offices of the county government or county seat.

Many colleges and universities with agricultural departments often issue separate bulletins on gardening, canning, freezing, storage, and so on. Your best bet is probably your state-supported university, although some private universities also freely distribute information.

The federal government distributes useful information. Write the Superintendent of Documents, Government Printing Office, Washington, D.C. 20250, for these publications:

"List of Available Publications of the USDA," Bulletin No. 11 (45 cents).

"Minigardens for Vegetables," H&G Bulletin No. 163 (15 cents).

Also write directly to the Publications Division, U.S. Department of Agriculture, Washington, D.C. 20250, for this publication:

"Suburban and Farm Vegetable Gardens," Bulletin No. G9 (free).

Glossary

ACID SOIL: *See p*H.

ALKALINE SOIL: *See p*H.

ANNUAL, plant that completes its life cycle in one growing season.

BACILLUS THURINGIENSIS: *See* Thuricide.

BLANCH, *1* to immerse (a vegetable) briefly in boiling water to stop enzyme action and thereby retard further flavor loss and toughening; *2* to bleach (a growing vegetable) by excluding light from it, as by drawing leaves over a cauliflower head to keep the buds white.

BLOOD MEAL, dried animal blood used for fertilizer. Its nitrogen content ranges from 9 to 15 percent.

BOLTING, going to seed, especially prematurely. Some cool weather plants, such as head lettuce, if exposed to high temperatures (70° to 80° F.), will not form heads but will undergo premature seeding and be useless as vegetables. Young cabbage will bolt at low temperatures (50° to 55° F.).

BONE MEAL, finely ground steamed animal bone used for fertilizer. It contains from 20 to 25 percent phosphoric acid and 1 to 2 percent nitrogen.

BREATHING, SOIL: *See* soil aeration.

CATCH CROPPING, planting quick-maturing vegetables in a plot where slow-maturing main crops have just been harvested. It may be done between plantings of main crops, or it may be done toward the end of a season, to utilize the last bit of frost-free time.

CLAY, soil composed of fine particles that tend to compact; it is plastic when wet but hard when dry. It takes water slowly, holds it tightly, drains slowly, and generally restricts water and air circulation.

COMPANION PLANTS, plants that influence each other, either beneficially or detrimentally. The influence may be chemical (odors or other exudates may have an effect), luminescent (a tall sun plant may protect a shade-loving low plant), etc.

COMPOST, mixture of loose vegetation, manure, or other once-living wastes that is left to decay through bacterial action and that is used for fertilizing and soil conditioning. Ripe compost is compost that has completed its decomposition and is ready for use.

COTTONSEED MEAL, ground cottonseeds used for fertilizer. It contains from 6 to 9 percent nitrogen, 2 to 3 percent phosphorus; and 2 percent potassium.

CROP ROTATION, growing different crops in a plot or field in successive years, usually in a regular sequence. Its purpose is to balance the drain on soil nutrients and to inhibit the growth of certain plant diseases. For nutrient preservation, for instance, heavy-feeding plants may be succeeded one year by plants that restore fertility to the soil; the following year light feeders may be planted. The next year heavy feeders may be planted again to begin the cycle anew.

CROP STRETCHING, any mode of vegetable planting that efficiently extends the use of a plot of ground. It may involve intercropping, succession cropping, or catch cropping (qq.v.); or it may involve the use of trellises, poles, or other devices to train plants in the air to save ground space.

CROWN, section of a plant at which stem and root merge.

CUTTING, section of a stem or root that is cut off and planted in a rooting medium (such as vermiculite or soil) so that it will sprout roots and develop into a plant that is similar in every respect to the parent plant. Nurseries sell powdered "rooting hormone" that encourages root growth for this purpose (directions for use are given on the package).

DORMANT, passing through a seasonal period of no active growth. Most perennials and other plants go dormant during the winter.

FISH EMULSION, liquid mixture containing discarded soluble fish parts, used as fertilizer. It contains usually 5 to 10 percent nitrogen and lesser amounts of phosphorus and potassium.

FLAT, shallow box in which seeds are planted to produce seedlings, generally indoors.

FRASS, sawdust-like refuse left behind by boring worms or insects. The term less commonly denotes the excrement left by insects.

FROND, leaf of a fern or palm; also, any fernlike leaf.

GERMINATION, sprouting of a new plant from seed.

GRANITE DUST, finely ground granite, used as a fertilizer. It contains about 8 percent potassium and a number of trace elements.

GREENSAND, sea deposit containing silicates of iron, potassium, and other elements, usually mixed with clay or sand. It contains 6 to 8 percent potassium and is used for fertilizer.

GYPSUM, mineral containing the soil nutrients calcium and sulfur and often used as a soil conditioner.

HARDENING (usually with *off*), getting an indoor-grown seedling used to outdoor weather by exposing it gradually to the outdoors.

HARDPAN, compacted clayey layer of soil that is impenetrable by roots and moisture. If near the surface, it can be spaded up and mixed with compost, manure, and other elements to make it more open, fertile, and hospitable to plants.

HEAVY FEEDER, any vegetable that absorbs large amounts of soil nutrients in the process of growth. Heavy feeders include cabbage, cauliflower, corn, cucumbers, leafy vegetables, rhubarb, and tomatoes.

HOT CAP, small waxed-paper cone that is set over an individual young plant to protect it from springtime cold. It is commercially made, one brand being called Hotkap.

HUMUS, black or brown decayed plant and animal matter that forms the organic part of soil.

INTERCROPPING, also called *interplanting*, planting quick-maturing and slow-maturing vegetables close together and then harvesting the quick-maturing ones before the slow-maturing ones have become big enough to overshadow or outcrowd them. Quick-maturing lettuce, for instance, can be seeded between beans.

LEACHING, dissolving nutrients or salts out of soil or fertilizer by the action of water percolating downward.

LEGUME, plant or fruit of a plant that bears edible pods, such as beans and peas. Legumes restore fertility to a soil by taking nitrogen compounds from the air and making them available in the soil.

LOAM, soil containing a fertile and well-textured mixture of clay, sand, and humus.

LIGHT FEEDER, any vegetable that requires small or moderate amounts of nutrients in the process of growth. Root crops are light feeders.

MANURE, livestock dung used as fertilizer. Fresh manure consists of recent excretions that have not decayed; it is generally unsuitable for direct application to soil in which plants are growing, but it is used in composting. Processed or rotted manure is decayed manure that is suitable for direct application as fertilizer.

MICROCLIMATE, sometimes called *miniclimate*, 1 climate from the surface of the soil to the top foliage of a plant; plants set close together overarch their leaves, creating trapped air beneath with moderate temperatures and less air flow; 2 uniform climate of a local site or geographical region.

MULCH, protective covering placed over the soil between plants. It may be peat moss, sawdust, compost, paper, opaque plastic sheeting, etc. Its purpose is to reduce evaporation, maintain even soil temperature, reduce erosion, and inhibit the sprouting of weeds.

NEMATODE, microscopic parasitic worm that infects plants and animals (phylum *Nematoda*).

NITROGEN, one of three most important plant nutrients, the others being phosphorus and potassium. It is particularly essential in the production of leaves and stems. An excess of nitrogen can produce abundant foliage and few flowers and fruit.

NUTRIENT, any of the sixteen elements that, in usable form, are absorbed by plants as nourishment. Plants obtain carbon, hydrogen, and oxygen from water and air, and the other elements from the soil. The main soil elements are nitrogen, phosphorus, and potassium; the trace elements are boron, calcium, chlorine, copper, iron, manganese, magnesium, molybdenum, sulfur, and zinc.

ORGANIC, deriving from living organisms, either plants or animals. In gardening, it denotes fertilizers or sprays of plant or animal origin, as opposed to those employing synthetic chemicals.

PEAT, prehistoric plant remains that have decayed under airless conditions beneath standing water, such as a bog. Peat moss, the most common form, is the remains of sphagnum moss. Its nutrient content is low—less than 1 percent nitrogen and less than 0.1 percent phosphorus and potassium; it is also highly acid. Added to the soil, it makes soil finer and more water-absorbent, but will also increase its acidity.

PEAT PELLET, small net-enclosed peat wafer that rises to six or seven times its original size on the addition of water. When expanded, it takes seeds, which develop into seedlings. Pellet and seedling together can be sown in the garden.

PEAT POT, tiny molded container made of peat, usually containing its own soil or planting medium. Seeds are planted in the pot, and seedling and pot together are transplanted to the soil outdoors. Pot shapes vary from cubes to truncated cones or pyramids.

PERENNIAL, plant that continues living over a number of years. It may die down to the roots at the end of each season but shoots up afresh every year. In areas of mild winters, the foliage may remain all year.

pH, index of the acidity or alkalinity of a soil. Technically, it refers to the relative concentration of hydrogen ions in the soil. The index ranges from 0 for extreme acidity to 7 for neutral, to 14 for extreme alkalinity. (The extremes, however, are rarely reached. A pH of 4.0 would be considered strongly acid; 9.0, strongly alkaline.) Soils in areas of heavy rainfall tend to be acid; those in areas of light rainfall tend to be alkaline. Adding peat moss, sawdust, or rotted bark to the soil increases acidity; adding lime increases alkalinity. Vegetables do best in a slightly acid soil, with a pH of 6.5 to 7.0; a safe range is 6.0 to 7.5.

PHOSPHORUS, one of the three most important plant nutrients, the others being nitrogen and potassium. It is especially associated with the production of seeds and fruits and with the development of good roots.

PINCHING, snipping off or shortening (shoots or buds) in order to produce a certain plant shape or to increase or decrease blooms or fruits. The snipping is done with finger and thumb Pinching the terminus of the main stem forces greater side branching. Pinching off the side shoots, conversely, stimulates more growth in the main stem, as well as in other remaining side stems.

POLLINATION, sexual reproduction in plants. Pollen, the fine dust produced by the male stamen of a flower, joins with the ovule of the female pistil of a flower, and the result is a seed to produce the next generation.

POTASSIUM, one of the three most important plant nutrients, the others being nitrogen and phosphorus. Its special value is to promote the general vigor of a plant and to increase its resistance to disease and cold. It also promotes sturdy roots.

POTASH, any potassium or potassium compound used for fertilizer. The potash in wood ash is potassium carbonate.

PYRETHRUM, insecticide made from the dried powdered flowers of certain plants of the *Chrysanthemum* genus. It is especially effective against aphids, leaf hoppers, caterpillars, thrips, and leaf miners.

ROCK PHOSPHATE, finely ground rock powder containing calcium phosphate. It contains up to 30 percent phosphoric acid. Superphosphate is rock phosphate that has been specially treated to yield phosphorus in various grades— 16, 20, or 45 percent. It also contains the nutrients calcium and sulfur.

ROTENONE, insecticide derived from the roots (and sometimes the stems) of certain New World tropical shrubs and vines of the genera *Derris* and *Lonchocarpus*. It is especially effective against beetles, caterpillars, leaf miners, thrips, aphids, and leaf hoppers.

RYANIA, insecticide made from the ground stems of a tropical South American shrub, *Patrisia pyrifera*. It is used especially against the corn borer.

SAND, tiny, water-worn particles of silicon and other rocks, each usually less than 2 millimeters in diameter. The granules allow free movement of air and water—so free, however, that water flows out readily and leaches out nutrients quickly.

SEEDLING, very young plant, especially one grown from seed.

SET, *1* small bulb, tuber, or root, or a section of a bulb, tuber, or root that is planted; *2* as a verb, often with *out*, to fix (a plant) in the soil, as in *to set out seedlings*.

SEWERAGE SLUDGE, sediment produced by sewage treatment processes and used as fertilizer. It contains about 5 percent nitrogen and 3 to 6 percent phosphorus and is usually sold under the trade name Milorganite.

SOIL AERATION, flow of oxygen and carbon dioxide within the soil, between the ground surface and plant roots and soil microorganisms. Plant roots absorb oxygen and release carbon dioxide (as opposed to plant leaves, which absorb carbon dioxide and release oxygen). Oxygen is also necessary to soil bacteria and fungi to decompose organic matter and produce humus.

SUBSOIL, bed of earthy soil immediately beneath the topsoil. The size of the soil particles may be larger than that of topsoil, sometimes approaching gravel size.

SUCCESSION PLANTING, planting a new crop as soon as the first one is harvested. This harvesting and re-planting in the same spot may occur more than once in a season, and it may involve the planting of the same vegetable or of different vegetables.

SUPERPHOSPHATE: *See* rock phosphate.

THINNING, pulling up young plants from a group so that the ones that are left in the soil have more room to develop properly.

THURICIDE, insecticide containing bacteria (*Bacillus thuringiensis*) that infect and kill several kinds of worms and caterpillars, without being toxic to plants or other animals.

TOPSOIL, surface layer of soil, containing fine rock particles and decayed or decaying organic matter. Its thickness varies from an inch or two to several feet, depending on the geographic region and past treatment of the soil.

VEGETABLE CLASSIFICATION, categorization of vegetables on the basis of the part of the plant that is used for food. Major root vegetables are beets, carrots, radishes, turnips and rutabagas. A common stem vegetable is asparagus. Major tuber vegetables are potatoes and yams. Major leaf and leafstalk vegetables are Brussels sprouts, cabbage, celery, endive, kale, lettuce, mustard greens, rhubarb, spinach, and Swiss chard. Major bulb vegetables are onions and garlic. The chief immature flowering vegetables are broccoli and cauliflower. Major vegetables that come as fruits (the seed-bearing parts) are beans, corn, cucumbers, eggplant, melons, okra, peas, peppers, squash, and tomatoes.

VERMICULITE, artificial planting medium consisting of inflated mica. It is highly water-absorbent and light-weight and is used mainly for growing seeds or plant cuttings. It can also be used to increase the water absorbency of soils.

WOOD ASH, burnt residue of wood, used as fertilizer. Its nutrient content varies greatly. Hardwood ash can contain as much as 10 percent potassium; softwood, as little as 2 percent. Exposure to rain can also leach out the nutrients. Wood ash runs high in lime (alkaline) content—sometimes as much as 40 percent lime.

Index

Gregg, Richard, 103

hardening transplants, 44
harvesting, 48-49. See also specific vegetables in Chapter 6
herbs, 8, 98-102, 104, 105, 106, 107-08
hot caps, 45
humus, 22

insecticides: See pesticides
insect predators (lacewing flies, ladybugs, praying mantises, trichogramma wasps), 111, 141
insects, 108, 109-21
intercropping, 45-46

kale, 72, 106

leafy vegetables, 8, 36
leeks, 112
legumes, 34
lettuce, 9, 73-75, 104, 105, 106, 107
loam, 22

manure, 23, 24-25, 29, 31, 33, 34
marigolds, 112, 113
marjoram, sweet, 99, 107
marjoram, wild: See oregano
maturity days for vegetables, 48-49. See also specific vegetables in Chapter 6
melons, 75-77, 105, 106
midget vegetables, 48
mint, 99, 108, 112
monoecious plant (cucumber), 67
moon cycles, planting by, 38-39
mustard greens, 78, 106

nasturiums, 106, 112
New Zealand spinach, 89
nitrogen, 22, 23-25, 105, 106, 130

okra, 79
onions, 80-81, 104, 106, 107, 108
oregano (origanum or wild marjoram), 100, 108
organic materials, vi, 4, 21-22, 23-25

parsley, 100, 106, 108
peas, 36, 81-83, 105, 106
peat pots, 43-44
peppers, 9, 84-85, 106
pesticides, 11-, 113-21
pests, garden, 109-21
Pfeiffer, E.E., 103
pH, 22-23
phosphorus, 23-25
planning the garden: See garden plans

planting indoors, 41-44. See also specific vegetables in Chapter 6
plant spacing, 39. See also specific vegetables in Chapter 6
potassium, 23-25
pyrethrum, 113-20

radishes, 85-87, 104, 105, 106, 112
rhubarb, 87-88
rock phosphate, 25
root vegetables, 8, 9, 36
rosemary, 100, 108, 113
rotenone, 120
Rototiller, (rotary tiller), 28-29
rutabagas, 96-97, 106
ryania, 120

sage, 101, 108, 113
sand, 22, 29, 30, 32
savory, 101, 106, 108
scallions, 80
seaweed, liquid, 25
seedlings, 41-45. See also specific vegetables in Chapter 6
seeds, 40-41, 42-45, 138-140. See also specific vegetables in Chapter 6
sewerage sludge, 25
soil, 20-23, 26
spacing of plants: See plant spacing
spinach, 88-89, 106
squash, 90-91, 105, 106
Steiner, Rudolf, v-vi, 103
storage of vegetables, 49
subsoil, 31-33
succession planting, 45-46
sunlight, 7
superphosphate: See rock phosphate
Swiss chard, 9, 92

tarragon, 101, 108
thinning, 41
Thuricide, 113
thyme, 101-102, 108
tomatoes, 93-96, 104, 106, 107, 108, 113
tools, 28
topsoil, 31-33
trailers: See vines
turnips, 96-97, 106

vines and trailers, 9, 105

warm and cool season plants, 35-37
watering, 34, 122-25
wood ash, 23, 25, 29, 31, 33, 34

zucchini, 90-91